Right Here

MOVING FROM A PRAYER LIFE

Right Now

TO A LIFE OF PRAYER

Jesus

The
Seedbed
Daily Text

Right Here

MOVING FROM A PRAYER LIFE

Right Now

TO A LIFE OF PRAYER

Jesus

Prayer

J. D. WALT

Unless otherwise noted Scripture quotations are taken from the Holy Bible, New International Version®, NIV® Copyright © 1973, 1978, 1984, 2011 by Biblica, Inc.™ Used by permission of Zondervan. All rights reserved worldwide. www.zondervan.com The "NIV" and "New International Version" are trademarks registered in the United States Patent and Trademark Office by Biblica, Inc.™ All rights reserved worldwide.

Scripture quotations marked ESV are from the ESV® Bible (The Holy Bible, English Standard Version®), copyright © 2001 by Crossway, a publishing ministry of Good News Publishers. Used by permission. All rights reserved.

Scripture quotations marked MSG are taken from *THE MESSAGE*, copyright © 1993, 1994, 1995, 1996, 2000, 2001, 2002 by Eugene H. Peterson. Used by permission of NavPress. All rights reserved. Represented by Tyndale House Publishers, Inc.

Printed in the United States of America

Cover illustration by
Cover and page design by Strange Last Name
Page layout by PerfecType, Nashville, Tennessee

Walt, John David.
  Right here right now, Jesus : moving from a prayer life to a life of prayer / J.D. Walt. – Franklin, Tennessee : Seedbed Publishing, ©2019.

        pages ; cm. – (Seedbed daily text)

        ISBN 9781628246735 (paperback)
        ISBN 9781628246742 (Mobi)
        ISBN 9781628246759 (ePub)
        ISBN 9781628246766 (uPDF)

        1. Prayer--Christianity. 2. Bible--Prayers. 3. Prayer--Biblical teaching.
        I. Title. II. Series.

BV215.W34 2019   248.3/2   2018967568

SEEDBED PUBLISHING
Franklin, Tennessee
seedbed.com

Contents

How the Daily Text Works

It seems obvious to say, but I write the Daily Text every day. I mostly write it the day before it is scheduled to release online.

Speaking of that, before we go further, I would like to cordially invite you to subscribe and receive the daily e-mail. Visit dailytext.seedbed.com to get started. Check out the weekly fasting challenge while you are there, and also the very active Facebook group.

Eventually, the daily postings become part of a Daily Text discipleship resource. That's what you hold in your hands now.

It's not exactly a Bible study, though the Bible is both the source and subject. You will learn something about the Bible along the way: its history, context, original languages, and authors. My goal is not educational in nature but transformational. I am more interested in our knowing Jesus than I am in our knowing *about* Jesus.

To that end, each reading begins with the definitive inspiration of the Holy Spirit, the ongoing, unfolding text of Scripture. Following this is a short and, hopefully, substantive insight from the text and some aspect of its meaning. For insight to lead to deeper influence, we turn the text into prayer. Finally, influence must run its course toward impact. This is why we ask each other questions. These questions are not designed to elicit information but to crystallize intention.

Discipleship always leads from inspiration to intention and from attention to action.

Using the Daily Text as a Discipleship Curricular Resource for Groups

While Scripture always addresses us personally, it is not written to us individually. The content of Scripture cries out for a community to address. The Daily Text is made for discipleship in community. This resource can work in several different ways. It could be read like a traditional book, a few pages or chapters at a time. Though unadvisable, the readings could be crammed in on the night before the meeting. Keep in mind, the Daily Text is not called the Daily Text for kicks. We believe Scripture is worthy of our most focused and consistent attention. Every day. We all have misses, but let's make every day more than a noble aspiration. Let's make it our covenant with one another.

For Use with Bands

In our judgment, the best and highest use of the Daily Text is made through what we call banded discipleship. A band is a same-gender group of three to five people who read together, pray together, and meet together to help one another grow into the fullness of Jesus Christ in this life. With banded discipleship, the daily readings serve more as a common text for the band and grist for the interpersonal conversation mill between meetings. The band meeting is reserved for the specialized activities of high-bar discipleship.

To learn more about bands and banded discipleship, visit newroombands.com. Be sure to download the free *Guide to Micro-Community Discipleship* or order a supply of the printed booklets online. Also be sure to explore our online platform for bands at app.newroombands.com.

For Use with Classes and Small Groups

The Daily Text has also proven to be a helpful disciple-ship resource for a variety of small groups, from community groups to Sunday school classes. Here are some suggested guidelines for deploying the Daily Text as a resource for a small group or class setting:

I. Hearing the Text

Invite the group to settle into silence for a period of no less than one and no more than five minutes. Ask an appointed person to keep time and to read the biblical text covering the period of days since the last group meeting. Allow at least one minute of silence following the reading of the text.

II. Responding to the Text

Invite anyone from the group to respond to the reading by answering these prompts: What did you hear? What did you see? What did you otherwise sense from the Lord?

III. Sharing Insights and Implications for Discipleship

Moving in an orderly rotation (or free-for-all), invite people to share insights and implications from the week's readings. What did you find challenging, encouraging, provocative, comforting, invasive, inspiring, corrective, affirming, guiding, or warning? Allow group conversation to proceed at will. Limit to one sharing item per turn, with multiple rounds of discussion.

Note: this resource comes with a free series of online streaming videos for each week's group meeting. In them, I share a seven- to ten-minute reflection on some aspect of the Scripture readings from the prior week. Some groups like to play the video at the beginning of this group sharing time as a way of kicking off the conversation.

IV. Shaping Intentions for Prayer

Invite each person in the group to share a single discipleship intention for the week ahead. It is helpful if the intention can also be framed as a question the group can use to check in from the prior week. At each person's turn, he or she is invited to share how their intention went during the previous week. The class or group can open and close their meeting according to their established patterns.

Introduction

I grew up on a farm. One of my most treasured memories happened in one of those hot and drought-stricken summers on the farm. Here I had watched my father and his men tirelessly and endlessly labor to raise those crops only to see them come to the brink of the disaster a drought can bring. If you know anything about farming or have ever been around it, you know the terrible feeling of that kind of injustice—giving your all and being brought to the brink of losing everything. I remember how he would load my two younger sisters, Missie and Erica, and I into the truck on some of those hot afternoons and drive us around the farm, field to field. As we circled each field he would lead us in loud singing, in a faith-filled way of praying for rain. Here was our song: *We need a rain. We need a rain. We need a rain. Have faith it will!*

When it really got desperate, Dad would interject in the midst of our song something like this: *We need a rain (about an inch and a half). We need a rain (about an inch and a half). We need a rain. Have faith it will!*

Like few others, farmers know they must work from sunup to sundown as though everything depended on their labor. At the end of the day, despite all their labor, farmers know the harvest does not depend on them, so they must pray as though everything depends on God. I think I learned more about prayer from the farm than I did the church. Maybe it's because the church taught prayer more from a place of duty and devotion. On the farm, we learned prayer from a place of dirt and desperation; not of the anxiety-ridden variety but a confident desperation—yes, even a holy desperation.

Over time, this way of holy desperation teaches us prayer is not so much a disciplined duty or fervent activity as it is a comprehensive way of walking with God. Prayer is neither preparation for the work, nor something we tack on after the work is done for good measure. Prayer becomes the very character and nature of the work itself.

It is easy to become confined by our prayers. We say these words at those times and at that place in the morning or before a meal or at this point in the Sunday service. Prayer slips into a faithful practice when it was meant to be the core substance of a faith-filled life. That's the point of this book— to shake us free from a dutiful prayer life and launch us into a more expansive life of prayer. It is moving from the practice of prayer as punctuation to the place where prayer flows freely as the everyday prose and occasional poetry of our lives.

At the core of this expansive prayer life is the beating heart of holy desperation. Nowhere do we see it more clearly than in Jesus Christ. His life reveals the picture of the holy desperation of unceasing prayer, a seamless way of life joining solitude and community, passion and power, seen and unseen, and through it all, heaven and earth.

> Then Jesus told his disciples a parable to show them
> that they should always pray and not give up. He said,

"In a certain town there was a judge who neither feared God nor cared what people thought. And there was a widow in that town who kept coming to him with the plea, 'Grant me justice against my adversary.'

For some time he refused. But finally he said to himself, 'Even though I don't fear God or care what people think, yet because this widow keeps bothering me, I will see that she gets justice, so that she won't eventually come and attack me!'"

And the Lord said, "Listen to what the unjust judge says. And will not God bring about justice for his chosen ones, who cry out to him day and night? Will he keep putting them off? I tell you, he will see that they get justice, and quickly. However, when the Son of Man comes, will he find faith on the earth?" (Luke 18:1–8)

Though I've loved this story for a long time now, I think I have missed its meaning for the most part. I think my former interpretation went like this: We're hopeless like that widow, but if we can get enough of us together in the same room enough times repeatedly asking for the same things, we can move God to do something. It's just another form of functional technology—of lever pulling—this time operating under the ironic auspices of widowhood.

We cite verses like, "if my people, who are called by my name, will humble themselves and pray and seek my face and turn from their wicked ways, then I will hear from heaven, and I will forgive their sin and will heal their land" (2 Chron. 7:14).

We trot them out like formulas or contracts, believing if we do our part then God is somehow in our debt to do his part, all the while forgetting the inconvenient truth that we owe God everything and God owes us nothing. The thought that human beings, by their actions, can somehow move or manipulate the actions of God is the height of self-deception and the very essence of idolatry. This idolatry shows itself by the way people commonly reference the power of prayer.

Can we call it? This parable is not about a powerless widow seeking power. It's about the judge. Truth be told, it's not even about the judge. It's about God. This parable is about God and how much our God is nothing like this unjust judge. This is our Abba who says, "I am the LORD your God, who brought you out of Egypt" (Exod. 20:2). This is our Abba, the one for whom nothing is impossible. This is our Abba, who liberally gives the Holy Spirit to those who ask. This is our Abba, who is slow to anger and rich in mercy, who is quick to forgive, whose steadfast love endures forever. This is our Abba, who says,

> Trust in the LORD and do good;
>> dwell in the land and enjoy safe pasture.
> Take delight in the LORD,
>> and he will give you the desires of your heart.
>
> Commit your way to the LORD;
>> trust in him and he will do this:
> He will make your righteous reward shine like the dawn,
>> your vindication like the noonday sun. (Ps. 37:3–6)

And though this world with devils filled is crawling with corrupt judges and treacherous men and women, this God hears the pleas of the widows and the cries of the orphans; indeed, not one sparrow falls to the ground that he does not know about (see Matthew 10:29).

Prayer is not powerful. God is powerful. Prayer doesn't change things. God changes things. Prayer merely opens up the pathway of faith that leads to the mysterious unfolding of God's will being "done on earth as it is in heaven" (Matt. 6:10). Just a few tracks back, Jesus' disciples made this request, "Increase our faith!" Jesus replied, "If you have faith as small as a mustard seed, you can say to this mulberry tree, 'Be uprooted and planted in the sea,' and it will obey you" (Luke 17:5–6).

Prayer has no power in and of itself. God alone has power. And somehow, faith mysteriously unlocks and unleashes the power of God on earth. So why does Jesus tell his disciples a parable to show them that they should always pray and not give up? Because prayer is the primary portal of faith and the primary practice of love. Prayer is the doorway into Jesus' relationship with his Abba. This is the house of God, which is the house of love, which is the place where miracles happen. Prayer is not a mechanistic movement or a dutiful discipline. It's an abiding place in which we dwell. You see, Jesus begins the lesson by talking about prayer, but look where he ends—"However, when the Son of Man comes, will he find faith on the earth?" (Luke 18:8).

Several years ago I spent part of my summer on the campus of Yale University in New Haven, Connecticut, at a conference studying the history of revival and awakening on the campuses of colleges and universities in this nation. It was a fascinating time. As we studied the historical accounts of the great awakenings in this country and beyond, it became clear they were all preceded by protracted seasons of passionate prayer. Historians refer to it as "travailing prayer." My friend and colleague, Dr. David Thomas, defines it as:

> a kind of spiritual posture found among some who were the catalytic core—a spirit of urgency and audacity, an attitude of brokeness and desperation, a manner of prayer that could be daring and agonizing. These friends in the Hebrides called it travailing prayer, like the Holy Spirit groaning through them, they said, like a woman travailing in labor, like Paul in Galatians 4:19 travailing "as if in the pangs of childbirth that Christ might be formed in you."

What amazed me most was how the participants in this gathering wanted to talk about prayer as strategy and in ways that felt highly functional and even technological. To them, prayer was like a massive lever and if we could get enough people to push, it would tip, moving the hand of God to do something. But what if it doesn't work that way? What if revival is really the tipping point of holy love in the community of God's people? And what if awakening were the massive shaking of the threshold of faith in the culture? Aren't these the real codes of "on earth as it is in heaven" faith working itself out in love? To historians, from the outside, it looks like a prayer movement. On the inside, it has all the makings of a God-birthed revolution of holy desperation begetting divine love in the world.

The real question Jesus asks us in this story is the one between the lines. It's not, "When the Son of Man comes, will he find faith on the earth?" (Luke 18:8). It's not, "Will not God bring about justice for his chosen ones, who cry out to him day and night?" (Luke 18:7). It's this one: Will God's chosen ones cry out to him day and night?

This brings us back around to the purpose of the book. Are we ready to move beyond a compartmentalized prayer life and into an expansive life of prayer? Is it time to graduate from quiet time and coffee to "cry out to him day and night"?

Jesus is calling his disciples beyond a mere prayer life and into an unbounded life of prayer. He wants to lead us to a radical kind of intimacy with God and each other that becomes the very labor and delivery room of the kingdom— the birthplace of divine love in the world. It's the place where prayer and justice and mercy and faith become inextricably intermingled and unleashed like a flood tide onto a parched land. It's a place where the dualisms of personal holiness and social holiness, the categories of "in here" and "out there," are collapsed and only the sheer unadulterated beauty of holy love remains. While prayer may not be the secret formula to a great awakening, we can be assured it paves the only pathway that will lead us there.

The pages ahead will encourage and embolden you, but they will also challenge and confound you. This is not a

INTRODUCTION

study in practice and technique. Though we will be anchored in orthodoxy, some of these reflections may strike you as unconventional and even unreasonable. It is the most difficult and challenging Daily Text series I have ever undertaken. Many were tempted to step away and some did.

We begin with the beginning, seeking to learn about prayer through the days of creation and the garden of Eden. We will end with a pensive walk through the recorded prayers of Jesus. I encourage you to stay with it and press in harder. While it may not be a beginner-level exploration of prayer, I believe it could save beginners from a lot of unlearning as they mature in faith.

As we begin this journey, let us all labor to enter in with a beginner's mind-set. Prayer is not ultimately a journey of learning, but of humility. There are no experts in the school of prayer. We live in desperate times. Let us climb in the truck together and survey the drought-stricken fields all around us as our Father leads us in the song of prayer: *We need a rain. We need a rain. We need a rain. Have faith it will!*

Right Here

MOVING FROM A PRAYER LIFE

Right Now

TO A LIFE OF PRAYER

Jesus

PART 1

Old Testament Prayers

Right Here. Right Now.

ACTS 1:4–11 | On one occasion, while he was eating with them, he gave them this command: "Do not leave Jerusalem, but wait for the gift my Father promised, which you have heard me speak about. For John baptized with water, but in a few days you will be baptized with the Holy Spirit."

Then they gathered around him and asked him, "Lord, are you at this time going to restore the kingdom to Israel?"

He said to them: "It is not for you to know the times or dates the Father has set by his own authority. But you will receive power when the Holy Spirit comes on you; and you will be my witnesses in Jerusalem, and in all Judea and Samaria, and to the ends of the earth."

After he said this, he was taken up before their very eyes, and a cloud hid him from their sight.

They were looking intently up into the sky as he was going, when suddenly two men dressed in white stood beside them. "Men of Galilee," they said, "why do you stand here looking into the sky? This same Jesus, who has been taken from you into heaven, will come back in the same way you have seen him go into heaven."

Consider This

As I begin this series on prayer, I want you, the reader, to know I am writing on a Thursday, exactly forty days after the Day of Resurrection. In other words, it is the Day of the Ascension of Jesus Christ. Whenever you happen to be starting, it bears noting that the major concerted movement of prayer in the New Testament begins on this day.

On this day, following Jesus' ascension, the disciples (120 of them) joined together in the Upper Room and met constantly in prayer until the Day of Pentecost. On the Day of Pentecost, we received the Holy Spirit, who would become the inspiration and source of our praying. The secret of prayer, however, takes us back to the ascension, which may be the most overlooked event in the history of history.

As we say in the great Creed of the Apostles: "He ascended into Heaven and sitteth at the right hand of God the Father Almighty."

I love how Timothy Tennent, who writes our Daily Text each Sunday, puts it. He says Jesus did not just ascend from here to there. Because he ascended into the heavens, he ascended from here to everywhere.

This is perhaps the first and most important teaching on prayer. We aren't sending our prayers "up there somewhere." We are speaking directly and immediately to the risen Son of God. Though unseen to the naked eye, he is right here, right now. Jesus is not with us in the sense that someone who can't come to our birthday party says they will be with us "in spirit." Jesus is not with us in spirit, but in person—in the power of the Holy Spirit.

The Great Commission Jesus gave his disciples ends with the words, "And surely I am with you always, to the very end of the age" (Matt. 28:20). By this he did not mean, "I'll be pulling for you in heaven." No, he meant *with you*. In fact, it is the very meaning of his name: Emmanuel—God with us.

The ascension of Jesus mysteriously means two completely different things all at the same time: he is high and lifted up. He is nearer than our breath. This makes prayer in the name of Jesus far more than the expression of human longing. Jesus raises prayer to the level of participation in the unfolding of the will of God—on earth as it is in heaven.

The ascension of Jesus Christ makes Christian prayer possible. To pray as a Christian does not mean, "I'll be thinking about you," as well-meaning people are prone to say when our life goes off the rails. It does not mean, "We will keep you in our thoughts and prayers," as the anchor person on the evening news casually repeats in the wake of unthinkable tragedy. To pray as a Christian means immediacy of access to Jesus, who is *right here, right now*.

I want you to deeply ponder those four words. They are the foundation on which everything else we will discuss concerning prayer stands.

Right here. Right now. Most people wait until the end of their life to finally discover this ultimate reality.

Discover it now.
Right here. Right now.

The Prayer

Lord Jesus, you are right here, right now. Even as I pray these words, I am aware I believe it more than I know it. I am ready to confess that I don't know what I don't know. Open the eyes of my heart that I might know you all at once high and exalted yet nearer than my breath. Right here, Jesus. Right now, Jesus. Amen.

The Questions

- In your prayer life do you tend to think of God as being somewhere out there or as immediately present?
- Do you find it easy or difficult to live in the awareness of Jesus' real presence with you, right here and right now?
- If Jesus really is right here, right now, wouldn't you want to grow more and more aware and attuned to this? What would that require on your part?

2 | The War of Prayer

ACTS 2:32–35 | God has raised this Jesus to life, and we are all witnesses of it. Exalted to the right hand of God, he has received from the Father the promised Holy Spirit and has poured out what you now see and hear. For David did not ascend to heaven, and yet he said, "'The Lord said to my Lord:

"Sit at my right hand until I make your enemies a footstool for your feet."'"

Consider This

Yesterday landed us in Acts 1 and the ascension of Jesus. Today we come to Pentecost and the church's first sermon. Didn't we say this series on prayer would begin with the Old Testament? Thanks for remembering.

The fascinating thing about today's text is that it contains the New Testament's most-quoted verse from the Old Testament: "The LORD says to my lord: 'Sit at my right hand until I make your enemies a footstool for your feet'" (Ps. 110:1). This verse appears at least six times in the New Testament.

Yesterday's text gave us the starting place for prayer: Jesus. Right here. Right now. Today's text gives us prayer's agenda and final destination: *until I make your enemies a footstool for your feet.*

These ten words form the agenda of "on earth as it is in heaven" (Matt. 6:10). The enemies of Jesus are Satan, evil, sin, death, and darkness, which show up in everything from oppression to opioid addiction, from cancer to child slavery, and from poverty to pornography.

To pray means to participate in the triumph—not of good over evil—but of Jesus over the evil one. Somehow and in some mysterious way, God chooses to win the battle through the participation of our prayers.

Jesus' primary vocation as he sits at the right hand of God is to pray. "Therefore he is able to save completely those who come to God through him, because he always lives to intercede for them" (Heb. 7:25). In fact, Jesus' primary vocation as he dwells among and within us is to pray. He prays without ceasing.

It would stand to reason that as we abide in him, we, too, pray without ceasing, and this not primarily because we are praying but because he is praying. Discipleship to Jesus means learning to pray in agreement with Jesus, in union with the mind of Christ. This does not come to us naturally. It must come supernaturally.

Sit at my right hand until I make your enemies a footstool for your feet.

Prayer means many things to many people. Biblically speaking, prayer means war. Prayer means advance. Prayer means recovering what has been lost and taking back what has been stolen. Remember in Ephesians how Paul closed his teaching on warfare in the Spirit? "And pray in the Spirit on all occasions with all kinds of prayers and requests. With this in mind, be alert and always keep on praying for all the Lord's people" (Eph. 6:18).

As I write this, I am leaning back in a leather chair with my feet propped up on a footstool. I'm thinking about Satan and evil and sin and darkness as that footstool. This is the vision. The way is made by the prayers of Jesus. The way is made by our participation with Jesus in that work. Wouldn't that be a welcome shift—from my prayer life to the prayer life of Jesus? That's where all this is heading.

The Prayer

Lord Jesus, you are right here, right now. And you will win the battle. I am sorry for always beckoning you to my side. I sense you saying it is time for me to come to your side. Show me the way beyond my own thin agenda that I might enter into your prayer life and step into the real battle where all you do is win. Right here, Jesus. Right now, Jesus. Amen.

The Questions

- What if we've missed the point of prayer? What if most of what we have learned about prayer is more shaped by culturally transmitted folk religion than the revealed Word of God?
- What is the significance of Psalm 110:1 and why do you think it appears so much in the New Testament?
- Is your prayer life lagging? What might it mean to join the prayer life of Jesus?

On the Necessity of Becoming a Beginner Again

3

JOHN 15:7–8 | "If you remain in me and my words remain in you, ask whatever you wish, and it will be done for you. This is to my Father's glory, that you bear much fruit, showing yourselves to be my disciples."

Consider This

The Christian vision of prayer is not empty-handed scar-city but overflowing fruit-full-ness. James said we have not because we ask not or we ask with wrong motives (see James 4:2–3). This is why the Word of God is so central to prayer. Jesus is not a wish genie but a prayer trainer. I like the way the psalmist put it, "He trains my hands for battle; my arms can bend a bow of bronze" (Ps. 18:34).

I see these weeks ahead as coming together before Jesus as humble students, as beginners even. We are asking him to interpret the Scriptures to us concerning prayer. One of my favorite prayers of Jesus is this one: "At that time Jesus said, 'I praise you, Father, Lord of heaven and earth, because you have hidden these things from the wise and learned, and revealed them to little children'" (Matt. 11:25).

I come to the task deeply mindful that I have learned a lot about prayer over the years and yet I am almost certain I know less about it than ever before. You too? In recent months, my own prayer life has grown tepid and tired. I think I am becoming teachable again.

The Prayer

Lord Jesus, you are right here, right now. Awaken my spirit by the presence of the Holy Spirit. Would you be my teacher? Would you train me in your way of prayer? School me in the ways of your Spirit. I am willing to start again in kindergarten. Right here, Jesus. Right now, Jesus. Amen.

The Questions

- Again, what if we've missed the point of prayer? What if most of what we have learned about prayer is more shaped by culturally transmitted folk religion than the revealed Word of God?
- How can we who have been walking with Jesus for many years approach him again as a beginner?
- What if prayer is less about a posture of empty-handed desperation and more about moving in faith-filled confidence of the answer of abundance?

In the Beginning: Prayer 4

GENESIS 1:1–3 | In the beginning God created the heavens and the earth. Now the earth was formless and empty, darkness was over the surface of the deep, and the Spirit of God was hovering over the waters. And God said, . . .

Consider This

Formless. Empty. Darkness. Deep.

Roll those four words around and off the tip of your tongue a few times, so your ears can hear them.

Formless. Empty. Darkness. Deep.

That's our problem. We spend far too much energy giving voice to the problem—to what is not. In doing so, we unwittingly magnify the status quo.

How often in the course of a single day do we give voice to and so amplify our problems? We speak of this family conflict and that work challenge and this sickness and that global ticking time bomb. It is as though we go around all day long speaking the words: *Formless. Empty. Darkness. Deep.*

We even try to convince others of just how formless, empty, dark, and deep the problems we face are.

Note who does not do this: God. The Bible does not begin with God rehearsing the problems of the not-yet universe. If God were to say, "formless, empty, darkness, and deep," it would only multiply them exponentially.

At the same time, the Bible does not deny this reality of nothingness. Just as rehearsing the reality does not reorder it, neither does denying the problem diminish it. The good news? Chapter 1 does not begin with verse 2. The key is verse 1.

In the beginning God created the heavens and the earth.

The biblical foundation for prayer begins neither with preexistent nothingness nor with broken everything. Our whole understanding and practice of prayer must begin with the beginning—Genesis 1:1. It means prayer begins with faith. Now, by *faith*, I don't mean to say the activity of human belief, but the reality of divine action. Faith is the willful decision of a community of people to live the totality of their existence in the light of God and in the world of God's making.

Faith is not asking and hoping. Faith means living in an alternative dimension of reality. What if the world we see with our eyes only comprises 10 percent of reality; or even 1 percent?

In the beginning God created the heavens and the earth.

No one ever talks much of the heavens, but what if the heavens make up the other 90 percent or 99 percent? What if the heavens and the earth were actually a seamless part of a unified whole? What if the fall of humanity breached this unity? And what if the life, death, resurrection, and ascension of Jesus Christ and the coming of the Holy Spirit inaugurated a new age wherein the heavens have broken in on the earth?

We understand these what-ifs as eternal verities, and these eternal verities are not our faith. They are *the* faith. As we get past our technical understanding of saying prayers, and seek to understand the deeper milieu of ultimate reality, prayer will take on enormous significance. It will, in fact, enter the realm of world-making. That's what prayer is—world-making speech. This is what God does. Remember now, the last three words of today's text.

And God said, . . .

The Prayer

Lord Jesus, you are right here, right now. I confess I so often give more focus to what is formless, empty, dark, and deep than to the God who created the heavens and the earth. My vision is limited by what I see instead of being anchored in the greater realm of the unseen. I welcome you to crush my thin categories, expand the horizons of my understanding, and blow my mind. Right here, Jesus. Right now, Jesus. Amen.

The Questions

- How do you find yourself magnifying formless, empty, darkness, and deep in your life? What would it take to stop this?
- Where do you put the percentages? What is seen versus what is unseen?
- What do you think of this understanding of prayer as learning to speak as God speaks?

5 The Three Most Powerful Words of Prayer

GENESIS 1:3–5 | And God said, "Let there be light," and there was light. God saw that the light was good, and he separated the light from the darkness. God called the light "day," and the darkness he called "night." And there was evening, and there was morning—the first day.

Consider This

What is prayer?

A prayer is a word or a series of words spoken in the power of the Spirit. We think of prayer as bringing our requests to God. I am growing to believe God sees prayer as learning to speak like God speaks.

Into the midst of the formless, empty, darkened depths God spoke words. Here we witness the Bible's first prayer. We will see it repeated several times in this opening chapter. It comes in at a whopping three words: *Let there be*.

The essence of these three short words can be distilled into a single word: *amen*. Amen means yes, we agree, let it be so. Isn't it just like God to begin the prayer in the way we typically end it?

Let there be light.

Amen, light!

Yes, it is like God to do this. Twenty-five times we see Jesus essentially begin what he says with, "Amen, amen I say unto you." Here's a fitting example: "In that day you will ask nothing of me. Truly, truly, I say to you, whatever you ask of the Father in my name, he will give it to you" (John 16:23 ESV).

This would mean prayer is less pleading and more calling forth.

Prayer, or speaking like God speaks, begins with incorporating these three words into our praying vocabulary: *"Let there be . . ."*

The world around us desperately needs people with the audacity to speak like God speaks; to speak words in the power of the Spirit into the formless, empty, dark, and deep situations. The world needs the followers of Jesus to become schooled and skilled with the creative speech of prayer.

Think of a difficult situation in your life right now. It could be in your family or at work or with a friend or colleague's life. I'm thinking of my twelve-year-old son, Sam. He's out of school for the summer. And he's already a bit lonely. He feels isolated. He came to give me a hug before bed last night, and he said, "Dad, I just want something to look forward to."

I've told you my tendency. It is to wade around in the formless, empty, dark depths of a situation. I want to learn to speak like God speaks instead. So I come before God, in the name of Jesus, embracing Sam and saying, "Amen! Amen! Let there be light. Let there be new friends. Let there be simple fun. Let there be flourishing faith. Let there be joy-inspiring plans for days ahead."

This challenges me. It might be a good challenge for you too. Give it a try.

Father, in the name of Jesus, in the power of the Spirit, as it comes to this situation _____, I say, "Amen! Amen! Let there be _____."

Speaking like God speaks. We may be onto something!

The Prayer

Lord Jesus, you are right here, right now. I confess the gravity of formless and empty holds me down. Darkness clings to me like a comfortable blanket. I want free of it, and I know it begins with learning to speak like you speak. Let there be awakening to the new possible. Right here, Jesus. Right now, Jesus. Amen.

The Questions

· What do you think about this notion of prayer as learning to speak like God speaks?

- How does this challenge your present conception of prayer? How are you challenged by leading with "Amen" and "Let there be"?
- How might you experiment with this approach? How might your intent to pray for someone become a practice of speaking like God might speak concerning them?

Why Prayer Doesn't Work and Who Does

6

GENESIS 1:6–8 | And God said, "Let there be a vault between the waters to separate water from water." So God made the vault and separated the water under the vault from the water above it. And it was so. God called the vault "sky." And there was evening, and there was morning—the second day.

Consider This

We see an interesting development in today's text. Yesterday, we saw this: "And God said, 'Let there be light,' and there was light" (Gen. 1:3).

Note the causality. God said. And there was. Note how today's text unfolds: *And God said, "Let there be a vault between the waters to separate water from water." So God made the vault and separated the water under the vault from the water above it.*

Did you catch the difference? *And God said, . . . So God made.* God followed his speaking with making. Sometimes prayer looks like creative speech. Other times, prayer looks like creative speech followed by creative action.

Imagine a long-neglected room in your home, a place you stuff everything you have no place for or otherwise don't know what to do with. The room has no windows and the lights no longer work. And did I mention the room is so full you can't walk inside. Now imagine one day, by force of habit, you go to the room to try and stuff in one more box of junk. You flip the light switch and, miracle of miracles, the room lights up. For all the glory of a working light, it only serves to expose the depths of the chaos. Formless, empty, no longer dark, but deeper than you imagined.

So God made the vault and separated the water under the vault from the water above it. And it was so. God called the vault "sky."

Light reveals the shape of the chaos. Now God speaks formation to that which was formless. He takes some of the water from the depths and places it in the heights and in between he creates space: atmosphere, if you will.

It's the same with our now-lit chaotic room. Miracle must lead to making, which requires moving, which leads to more miracles (like finding your long-lost engagement ring and the file containing your kids' birth certificates). Only now you discover you are pregnant again (a word of prophecy for some of you out there), and this room you had formerly written off as formless chaos begins to take on all sorts of new possibilities in your mind's eye.

Let's call it, "blue sky."

Sometimes God moves mountains in an unmistakably sovereign way. More often, he moves us, by the strength of his Spirit, to move all the old furniture out of the chaotic storage room. Sometimes a word will get it done. Other times to that word we must add rolling up our sleeves. It's all God, though. And all good.

This is how prayer, a.k.a. "creative speech," works. Okay, prayer doesn't work. This is how God works, which is what prayer is.

The Prayer

Lord Jesus, you are right here, right now. I am overwhelmed by the chaos around me. Yet I suspect my feelings of being overwhelmed have more to do with the chaos within me. Reveal to me the creative words you are speaking over me and give me the grace to echo them out loud. Sort the junk drawers and closets in my soul. Then I might see clearly to help others with theirs. Right here, Jesus. Right now, Jesus. Amen.

The Questions

- Where does your mind run in response to today's text? Do you see more problems or more possibilities?
- Are you beginning to see how prayer is far more than prayers, that it is a new and powerful way of life and being in the world?

- About that room we talked about: What and where is that in your life? What is God speaking over and around that place?

7 | The True Way of Prayer Is Claim It and Name It

GENESIS 1:9–10 | And God said, "Let the water under the sky be gathered to one place, and let dry ground appear." And it was so. God called the dry ground "land," and the gathered waters he called "seas." And God saw that it was good.

Consider This

Yesterday, we witnessed the God who prays work through word and deed. I started to say word and action and stopped myself. God's Word is action. Scripture tells us it is "alive and active" (Heb. 4:12). We are so casual with our words, failing to realize the sheer power they carry.

Friendly reminder: We are created in the image of a God "[who] speaks and listening to his voice new life the dead receive!" (Charles Wesley says, "You're welcome," for that gem.) To pray means to speak after God, or in the way God speaks.

Maybe this is the most fundamental insight of all: God prays. Who does God pray to? Himself. We have no trouble grasping the notion of Jesus praying, yet it seems a bit odd to think of God as praying. But what if we've got the whole concept of praying wrong? We think of prayer primarily as something we do. What if prayer is primarily something God does? What if, in fact, true prayer is a participation in the dialogue of the heavens, joining into the creative conversation of God—Father, Son, and Holy Spirit?

There's a difference between saying prayers and praying. Saying prayers can train us for praying, but praying requires more than this. It requires the long, slow cultivation of a memory steeped in Scripture, an attentiveness anchored in the embodied humanness of Jesus (which is our humanity), and an imagination fired by the Holy Spirit and imbued with all the possibilities of the kingdom of heaven.

To today's text—note how God speaks prescriptively: *Let the water under the sky be gathered to one place, and let dry ground appear.* Note their effect: *And it was so.* Now note how God follows this by speaking descriptively: *God called the dry ground "land," and the gathered waters he called "seas."*

God's sacred speech, also known as prayer, first creates atmosphere, breathing space. Next, God creates habitat, or living space. In this way, prayer brings forth a new kind of order, which is itself bursting forth with a generative creativity. To pray is to speak prescriptively into the formless, empty chaos, and then to speak descriptively as new creation begins to emerge.

Rather than the counterfeit way of "name it and claim it," prayer, or speaking after God, is just the opposite: claim it and name it. Permit me to ponder this at a high level of analogy.

Prayer begins by claiming the formless, empty, dark depths—from which we typically want to run. The prayer, "Let there be light," reveals the shape and illumines the nature of the chaos we face. Prayer proceeds to create atmosphere and then habitat—environmental conditions from which many other new things can spring forth.

The movement of prayer is from prescribing to describing, from claiming to naming. There is yet another movement of prayer from today's text. It may be the most important one so far.

And God saw that it was good.

Let's call it surveying and celebrating.

Whose ready to go claim some chaos out there today?

The Prayer

Lord Jesus, you are right here, right now. Thank you for not fleeing the chaos, but running straight into the middle of it. Bring me inside of your prayer life. Show me the ways you want to claim the chaos around me and within me, and walk me through what it looks like to speak into it and act upon it. Though I'm out of my depths, I know this is the shallow end for you. Right here, Jesus. Right now, Jesus. Amen.

The Questions

- How does the idea of prayer being something God does and we participate in impact your understanding and approach to prayer?

- How do you see ways that prayer can create atmosphere (breathing space) and habitat (living space) for the creative, generative work of God?
- How are you claiming the chaos around you? Within you? What is the Holy Spirit leading you to prescribe through prayer into that chaos? How do you describe ways God has brought creative order in the past? How are you surveying and celebrating progress?

Why Prayer Does Not Move God and What Does

8

GENESIS 1:14–19 | And God said, "Let there be lights in the vault of the sky to separate the day from the night, and let them serve as signs to mark sacred times, and days and years, and let them be lights in the vault of the sky to give light on the earth." And it was so. God made two great lights—the greater light to govern the day and the lesser light to govern the night. He also made the stars. God set them in the vault of the sky to give light on the earth, to govern the day and the night, and to separate light from darkness. And God saw that it was good. And there was evening, and there was morning—the fourth day.

Consider This

We see another pattern playing out through these days of creation.

And there was evening, and there was morning—the fourth day.

First, I find it interesting we tend to think of days as running from morning to evening. The Bible says days run from evening to morning. In other words, the biblical day does not begin with a sunrise, but a sunset. With God, day begins with night. God does not sleep. When we go to sleep, God goes to work. We awaken into the work of God in progress.

Wandering Israel went to bed. God went to work. They awakened to manna already on the ground. There is a word concerning prayer here. To pray is never to initiate the work of God or to somehow move God to act. God is the initiator, always working. Our praying is always a response to God's prior initiative. In fact, prayer is the most ready (if not the only) pathway into the activity of God. We often say in our work with Seedbed, "Prayer is not the only thing we do, but it is the first thing."

And there was evening, and there was morning—the fourth day.

It's interesting it doesn't say day and night, but evening and morning. Also fascinating is the way evening and morning have been the appointed times of prayer throughout all the ages, from Israel to the present-day church.

Many believe God is moved by our prayers. It is the gateway to idolatry, the tragic notion that we can somehow determine the activity of God. God is not moved by prayer but by love. In fact, prayer is the great school of love, where we experience the movements of the gospel—from God to self, from self to God, and with God to others.

I like the way E. M. Bounds said it, "God shapes the world by prayer. . . . The prayers of God's saints are the capital stock in Heaven by which Christ carries on his great work upon the earth."[1]

A further word about chaos and prayer. Because to pray is to love, prayer means entering into and even embracing the chaos. While we might say prayers about given chaotic situations, we are only truly praying to the extent we are willing to claim the chaos. This is why prayer is a costly thing.

To tell another person, "I'll be praying for you," is a serious thing. It is not sitting passively and sympathetically on the outside, speaking words to God on their behalf. Rather, it means something more like, "I will stand with Jesus for you in the midst of the chaos." Real praying is not human-inspired sympathy but Spirit-empowered empathy.

The great Adoniram Judson said it best, "You can do more than pray, after you have prayed, but you can never do more than pray until you have prayed."

The Prayer

Lord Jesus, you are right here, right now. You have claimed our chaos, and day by day you are sorting it out. Draw me into this work and bring my praying into alignment with yours. Increase my praying not by the strength of my own

---

1 E. M. Bounds, *E. M. Bounds on Prayer* (Peabody, MA: Hendrickson Publishers, 2006), 172.

commitment and determination, but by the power of your love. Right here, Jesus. Right now, Jesus. Amen.

The Questions
- How often do you tell someone you are praying or will pray for them? How often do you really do it?
- What do you think about the statement, "God is not moved by prayer, but by love"? How does prayer figure into this?
- How might this evening-to-morning movement influence and even inspire your prayer practices?

9 | Why Prayer Is Not the Solution to Our Problem

GENESIS 1:20–25 | And God said, "Let the water teem with living creatures, and let birds fly above the earth across the vault of the sky." So God created the great creatures of the sea and every living thing with which the water teems and that moves about in it, according to their kinds, and every winged bird according to its kind. And God saw that it was good. God blessed them and said, "Be fruitful and increase in number and fill the water in the seas, and let the birds increase on the earth." And there was evening, and there was morning—the fifth day.

And God said, "Let the land produce living creatures according to their kinds: the livestock, the creatures that move along the ground, and the wild animals, each according to its kind." And it was so. God made the wild animals according to their kinds, the livestock according to their kinds, and all the creatures that move along the ground according to their kinds. And God saw that it was good.

Consider This

I never imagined the creation account would teach me so much about the life and ways of prayer. Honestly, I never considered it as part of the curriculum. Why is that?

We consider prayer as a post-fallen Eden reality. We approach prayer as a way to solve a problem—a response to sin, darkness, and death. In fact, we approach most all of Christian faith this way—as a solution to the problem of sin. For all practical purposes, our Bible begins with Genesis 3.

What if Christian faith is not merely God's solution to man's problem? What if, in fact, Christian faith is the true nature and shape of ultimate reality, which is not sin, darkness, and death, but unfettered flourishing?

If there is a word to describe Genesis 1 it would be *flourishing*. "The land produced vegetation: plants bearing seed according to their kinds and trees bearing fruit with seed in it according to their kinds. And God saw that it was good" (Gen. 1:12).

Now, note the flourishing in today's text: *God blessed them and said, "Be fruitful and increase in number and fill the water in the seas, and let the birds increase on the earth." . . . And God said, "Let the land produce living creatures according to their kinds: the livestock, the creatures that move along the ground, and the wild animals, each according to its kind."*

To restate my working assumption: Prayer is divine speech. It is the working Word of God to call forth the things that are not as though they were and the releasing of everything for the fulfillment of its creational intent, which is the flourishing of abundant life.

Prayer is a participation in this kind of work. Flash-forward to this instructive word from God in the New Testament, "If you remain in me and my words remain in you, ask whatever you wish, and it will be done for you. This is to my Father's glory, that you bear much fruit, showing yourselves to be my disciples" (John 15:7–8).

To be sure, we live as fallen creatures in the midst of a fallen creation. We, however, are called to arise into the post-resurrection reality of our ascended Lord, where the new creation of the kingdom of heaven bursts at the seams to break in upon the broken order and renew the flourishing of all abundance.

This is prayer, not as a reaction or even response to sin, darkness, and death, but as co-creative participation in the word and work of God to renew all of creation.

Let's be clear. Jesus is not wringing his hands at the right hand of God, trying to fix broken things. Jump from the first book to the last where we read, "And he who was seated on the throne said, 'Behold, I am making all things new'" (Rev. 21:5 ESV).

Not *I will*, but *I am*.

To these things, we must awaken.

The Prayer

Lord Jesus, you are right here, right now. You are not patching things up. You are making them new again. Open my mind to what *new* means. Open my heart to what *new* could be. Fill us with the fullness of original flourishing. And let it be with me. And let me be a participant in this work with you. Right here, Jesus. Right now, Jesus. Amen.

The Questions

- What is your vision of the word *flourishing*? What would original flourishing look like in your life, family, relationships, marriage, work, school, church, town?
- Do you tend to frame reality with the problem of sin, darkness, and death or are you reaching for that larger faith framework of original flourishing? How does that change things for you?
- How is this changing the way you understand and practice prayer? Name one clear and practical way forward with this.

How Prayer Leads Us into a Whole New World | 10

GENESIS 1:26–28 | Then God said, "Let us make mankind in our image, in our likeness, so that they may rule over the fish in the sea and the birds in the sky, over the livestock and all the wild animals, and over all the creatures that move along the ground."

So God created mankind in his own image, in the image of God he created them; male and female he created them.

God blessed them and said to them, "Be fruitful and increase in number; fill the earth and subdue it. Rule over the fish in the sea and the birds in the sky and over every living creature that moves on the ground."

Consider This

A lot of believers report being challenged deeply to think about prayer in these unexplored ways. Others report blown mental circuitry with appreciation. A few are ready to quit because it doesn't make sense. I want you to know I appreciate and validate all of that. Please know I am only trying to go where the text leads me.

It's fair also at this point to recognize I am not speaking of prayer in the usual fashion. We are crafting a theology of prayer by beginning at the beginning. We are not so much asking the Holy Spirit to teach us something new or novel about prayer as much as we are asking him to reveal to us what has been there all along, yet perhaps unnoticed. Admittedly, we are not yet dealing with prayer in a functional or technical sense. Rather, we are dealing with it at the level of its deepest essence and nature.

When it comes to prayer, most of us don't need to try harder. What we need is a deeper understanding. We don't need a change in method as much as we need a change in mind-set. That is where I am coming from. If you are struggling, I urge you to lean in and bear with me a bit longer. We will drink the water soon enough. For now, it is important that we dig the well deeper.

My first fundamental shift comes with what prayer even is. Up to this point I would have considered prayer as words we say to God. I now understand prayer as divine speech. In the same way Jesus prays in John 11:

> And Jesus lifted up his eyes and said, "Father, I thank you that you have heard me. I knew that you always hear me, but I said this on account of the people standing around, that they may believe that you sent me." When he had said these things, he cried out with a loud voice, "Lazarus, come out!" (vv. 41–43 ESV)

God prays in Genesis 1, "Let there be light" (v. 3).

We are told in Paul's letter to the Romans about the Holy Spirit praying: "In the same way, the Spirit helps us in our weakness. We do not know what we ought to pray for, but the Spirit himself intercedes for us through wordless groans" (8:26).

Before prayer is ever human speech, it is divine speech.

Bringing it to today's text: to be created in the image and likeness of God must have something to do with some manner of speaking like God speaks. After all, we get twenty-five verses of God speaking creation out of chaos, after which we are told we are created in the image of this God. In fact, he created us so we might rule the creation. It would stand to reason that God would intend the creation to be ruled in the same way it was created, by the will and word of God.

In all of creation, it appears only men and women have the capacity to speak like God speaks. Remember Ezekiel as he was instructed to speak to the bones and to the breath. God commanded Ezekiel to prophesy, which is a manner of praying and means to speak like God speaks (see Ezekiel 37:1–14).

What if our most powerful and creative capacity as image-bearers of God is to speak like God speaks—to pray? Could this be what it means to rule like God rules—to walk with God in the ways of God, by the will of God, and in accordance with the Word of God? I am becoming convinced that this is what prayer means.

This creation mandate in Genesis 1 for the image-bearers of God to rule over creation effectively makes us viceroys—a ruler exercising authority on behalf of a sovereign. If I'm honest, my praying comes more from a place of victimization than viceroy. I live too much as a victim of sin, darkness, and death, and what I call prayer is too often the amplification of my anxieties to God. Surely, prayer must mean more than this.

For years now I have been mesmerized by something the late Henri Nouwen wrote concerning prayer. Let's give him the last word today.

> The word "prayer" stands for a radical interruption of the vicious chain of interlocking dependencies that leads to violence and war, and for an entering into a totally new dwelling place. It points to a new way of speaking, of breathing, of being together, of

knowing—truly, to a whole new way of living. . . . Prayer is the center of the Christian life. It is living with God, here and now.[2]

The Prayer

Lord Jesus, you are right here, right now. Teach us to pray. I am far more at home in learning about what I think I already know. I need to come clean and confess I know very little of this divine mystery. I want to be teachable. I am ready to be stretched. I look to you. Right here, Jesus. Right now, Jesus. Amen.

The Questions

- Are you finding yourself frustrated with this series on prayer so far? Can you stay with the struggle a bit longer? What would help you?
- How do you feel stuck in your present understanding and practice of prayer? Do you sense yourself getting unstuck? How?
- What do you make of this distinction between a victim and a viceroy when it comes to prayer? Where do you see yourself?

---

2   John Dear, ed., Henri J. M. Nouwen, *The Road to Peace: Writings on Peace and Justice* (Maryknoll, NY: Orbis Books, 1998), n.p.

11 Why We Must Rest from Prayer

GENESIS 2:2–3 | By the seventh day God had finished the work he had been doing; so on the seventh day he rested from all his work. Then God blessed the seventh day and made it holy, because on it he rested from all the work of creating that he had done.

Consider This

When my children were younger we initiated a practice of Sabbath-keeping in our home. It was not so much a day of don'ts as the practice has tended to become throughout history. Rather, Sabbath meant a day of dos; of doing things we didn't do on other days. We learned the four major practices or movements of Sabbath from Marva Dawn's marvelous book *Keeping the Sabbath Wholly: Ceasing, Resting, Embracing, Feasting*. We composed a short rhyming prayer and each Saturday night around bedtime we would light our Sabbath lamp and recite it together.

God give us your peace, and cause us to rest. We cease from our labor. We seek for your best. Embracing each other, we walk in your ways. We thank you for giving this new Sabbath day.

As we kept this simple ritual we found it kept us. I used to think Sabbath-keeping was all about revving up the devotional engines, a day for more prayer in order to prepare for the busy workweek ahead. I understand it differently now. Sabbath-keeping means entering into the rest of God.

Keeping Sabbath holy is all about realignment and reorientation around the holiness of God: Father, Son, and Holy Spirit. Sabbath resets the pattern of creation days, which, remember, begin at night. Sabbath restores our fundamental identity as sons and daughters, tangibly reminding us we are no longer slaves. Rather than being compelled by a master to work, we are compelled by our Maker to rest.

The nature of Sabbath rest is very different from the typical idea of rest. We primarily think of rest as preparatory. We rest because we are tired, or we rest up for the work ahead. These notions of rest are functional and utilitarian and quite foreign to the rest of God. Though these are clearly human needs, God does not need to rest in these ways. The rest of God reminds us that rather than being defined by our work we can be delighted with God both in and through our work. And, remember, to the extent we can grasp that our work is prayer, God will weave his will into and out of our work—no matter what our particular job happens to be.

Lest we forget, the last word in the Genesis 1 creation account is, "God saw all that he had made, and it was very good" (v. 31). On the seventh day, God ceased from his creative speech and action. Rather than making anything, he made something he created holy—not the creation, but time itself. "Then God blessed the seventh day and made it holy, because on it he rested from all the work of creating that he had done" (Gen. 2:3).

God calls us over and over, week after week, to set apart space to recover the gifted holiness of time. It happens through taking delight in the exceptional gift of God with us, the extraordinary gift of the people around us, and the very good gift of the creative and redemptive work behind us.

So what does all of this have to do with prayer? Let me test this theo-logic. If prayer is our work, and Sabbath is a day to rest from work, wouldn't it mean Sabbath is a day to rest, even from our prayers? How about if we allowed our Sabbath prayers to shift from the character of work to the posture of resting in the gift of God's presence?

Let's give Oswald Chambers the last word today: "Prayer does not fit us for the greater works; prayer *is* the greater work."[3]

The Prayer

Lord Jesus, you are right here, right now. So often we try to bring you into the yoke of what holds us back. Instead you call us to "take my yoke upon you" where you would show us a way of life that fits, that is easy and even light (Matt. 11:29–30). We sense this new way of work is actually a new way of prayer. Open for us a new and living way of prayer where we might find this easy yoke. We long for this. Right here, Jesus. Right now, Jesus. Amen.

---

3   Oswald Chambers, *My Utmost for His Highest* (New York: Dodd Mead, 1940), October 17.

The Questions

- How do you understand and interpret the Oswald Chambers's quote in your own words and experience?
- How does this teaching on Sabbath challenge your former ways of thinking? Where do you sense the Holy Spirit's invitation to you in it?
- Does your life and identity tend to be shaped and defined according to labor and leisure? How might Sabbath reshape those categories?

Several years back I did a deep dive of research and study into the biblical practice of Sabbath-keeping. I captured my learnings in a short book called *Sabbath Keeping: It's About Time*. For those who are interested in this Seedbed Seedling, you can download it at no charge from seedbed.com.

The Epic Fail of Eden 12

GENESIS 3:1–6 | Now the serpent was more crafty than any of the wild animals the LORD God had made. He said to the woman, "Did God really say, 'You must not eat from any tree in the garden'?"

The woman said to the serpent, "We may eat fruit from the trees in the garden, but God did say, 'You must not eat fruit from the tree that is in the middle of the garden, and you must not touch it, or you will die.'"

"You will not certainly die," the serpent said to the woman. "For God knows that when you eat from it your eyes will be opened, and you will be like God, knowing good and evil."

When the woman saw that the fruit of the tree was good for food and pleasing to the eye, and also desirable for gaining wisdom, she took some and ate it. She also gave some to her husband, who was with her, and he ate it.

Consider This

Now the serpent . . . perhaps the three most foreboding words in the Bible.

The serpent, a.k.a. Satan, begins by calling the word of God into question.

"Did God really say, 'You must not eat from any tree in the garden'?"

This serpent, we are told, is most crafty. Note the not-so-subtle distortion in the reframing of God's word. Now hear the woman's response:

"We may eat fruit from the trees in the garden,"

So far so good.

"but God did say, 'You must not eat fruit from the tree that is in the middle of the garden'"

Still batting a thousand.

"'and you must not touch it, or you will die.'"

At this point I hear in my mind the fail music they play on *The Price Is Right* when someone fails the challenge. It's too bad this was a pass/fail test with no partial credit. She got two-thirds of it exactly right. For the record, here's what God actually said: "And the LORD God commanded the man, 'You are free to eat from any tree in the garden; but you must not eat from the tree of the knowledge of good and evil, for when you eat from it you will certainly die'" (Gen. 2:16–17).

It's also worth pointing out that God didn't actually say this to the woman but to Adam. Chances are, Adam gave Eve his translation, or worse, his sense of what God said. Regardless, someone got it wrong, which shows us the high-stakes nature of biblical work. Bottom line: Satan reads Scripture, too, and some of the worst atrocities in human history have occurred as a consequence of his distorted reading of the text.

Note also the deeper craft of Satan's crafty-ness: *Did God really say, 'You must not eat from any tree in the garden'?"* He deploys a scare tactic; more properly, a scarce tactic. He creates the appearance of scarcity, and the suggested appearance of scarcity creates the experience of scarcity. (Scarcity is not an external fact but an internal effect. Scarcity is what makes the rich hoard and the poor beg.) The experience of scarcity arises from the presence of fear, which comes from the failure of trust, and the failure of trust comes from a loss of confidence in the trustworthiness of the one being trusted: in this case, God.

So what does any of this have to do with prayer? Everything. How we understand God determines how we see ourselves, and how we see ourselves determines how we experience the world. Do we experience the world from a place of abundance or scarcity? This will determine how we pray.

When we live in scarcity, we pray like beggars. Meanwhile, Jesus says stuff like, "If you, then, though you are evil, know how to give good gifts to your children, how much more will your Father in heaven give good gifts to those who ask him!" (Matt. 7:11).

Do we really believe God wants us to approach him as beggars? Does anyone out there want their children to approach them as beggars?

Whether you want to lean in with me on this way of seeing God's speech in creation as prayer or not, this tour through these opening chapters of the Bible is meant to help us locate ourselves. Are we Genesis 1–2 people flourishing in abundance or are we Genesis 3 scarcity people? The resurrection and ascension of Jesus and the coming of the Holy Spirit doesn't all at once abolish the reality of Genesis 3; however, it opens a new and living way of prayer anchored far more in the possibilities of Eden and the new creation than in the problems of exile.

Whether we will admit it or not, most of us have become quite comfortable living in scarcity. It is, after all, predictable. To live into the abundant kingdom of heaven is risky business.

The Prayer

Lord Jesus, you are right here, right now. I must look like a fool in all my begging when you hold out the riches of your kingdom as a pure gift. Lead me into the new and living way you opened up. Teach me to live into this inheritance in ways

RIGHT HERE. RIGHT NOW.

that extend it to others. I want to learn to pray like that. Right here, Jesus. Right now, Jesus. Amen.

The Questions
- The real question is not whether you are rich or poor but are you a scarcity or an abundance person?
- What insight do you take away from these early chapters of Genesis?
- How might you practically begin to move in the faith of flourishing?

Prayer *as* Walking with God vs. Prayer *Is* Walking with God

13

GENESIS 3:8–9 | Then the man and his wife heard the sound of the LORD God as he was walking in the garden in the cool of the day, and they hid from the LORD God among the trees of the garden. But the LORD God called to the man, "Where are you?"

Consider This
God walks.

God walks in the garden.

God walks in the garden in the cool of the day.

God walks in the garden in the cool of the day with Adam and Eve.

We can assume this is the creational intent of the Creator—to walk with his image-bearers. Is this not what prayer is in its deepest essence: walking with God? We think of prayer as talking to God. If we are honest, though, we must admit we largely think of prayer as talking to God from a distance. We pray to a God who we sense is with us, just not really here. God is somewhere else.

Here's the interesting thing about walking. It seems obvious to say, but you can only walk with someone you are actually with. So here's the question: What if before prayer is talking to God, it is walking with God? Walking with God is not a metaphor for prayer. It is prayer.

Prayer is walking with God in a garden in the cool of the day. The lyrics from the chorus of the well-known hymn "In the Garden" come to mind, "And he walks with me and he talks with me and he tells me I am his own." This is the essence of prayer—walking with and talking with God.

Remember the creedal declaration with which this series began? "He ascended into Heaven and sitteth at the right hand of God the Father Almighty." Because Jesus ascended to the right hand of God, he did not merely ascend from here to there, but from here to everywhere. And as you have undoubtedly noticed, our daily prayer now begins and ends by affirming the right here, right now presence of Jesus.

This cannot be overstated. Prayer, or as Jesus called it, "abiding," can no longer mean speaking words to a deity somewhere out there. It must mean walking and talking with the God who is both transcendently present "at the right hand of God the Father Almighty," and immanently by our side, closer than our breath. Indeed, this is pure mystery and yet it is the ultimate and immediate reality. To walk by faith—there it is again—means to live in this very real place called prayer.

So much of what we call prayer, from casual recitations to intense incantations, is not only less than, but categorically different from what the Bible means concerning prayer. We settle for so much less than the flourishing abundance set before us. On that point, let's give the venerable C. S. Lewis the last word today. Here's an unforgettable quote from the opening volley of his celebrated sermon, "The Weight of Glory":

> We are half-hearted creatures, fooling about with drink and sex and ambition when infinite joy is offered us, like an ignorant child who wants to go on making mud pies in a slum because he cannot imagine what is meant by an offer of a holiday at the sea. We are far too easily pleased.[4]

As the old hymn "In the Garden" says, "And the joy we share as we tarry there . . ."

The Prayer

Lord Jesus, you are right here, right now. Forgive us for spiritualizing your presence when you are more present and available to us now than before you ascended. Give me the

4 C. S. Lewis, *The Weight of Glory and Other Addresses* (New York: HarperCollins, 1976), 26.

spirit of wisdom and revelation that I might know you better. Awaken me to your very real presence. I quite literally want to walk with you. Right here, Jesus. Right now, Jesus. Amen.

The Questions
- God walking in the garden in the cool of the day. Is it a mythological notion or a concrete reality in your understanding?
- Walking with God. Is it a nice, lofty ideal for you or a growing, tangible reality? How might physically walking for prayer aid this growing reality?
- How would you describe your discontent with your present reality of a daily walk with God? How would you describe your aspiration? How might the reality grow?

14 On the Difference between a Prayer Life and a Life of Prayer

GENESIS 4:25–26 | Adam made love to his wife again, and she gave birth to a son and named him Seth, saying, "God has granted me another child in place of Abel, since Cain killed him." Seth also had a son, and he named him Enosh.

At that time people began to call on the name of the Lord.

RIGHT HERE. RIGHT NOW.

Consider This

We find ourselves in the first generation of grandchildren who are the second generation of people who have no direct memory of Eden. Perhaps the experience of walking with God had been shared with Cain and Abel and later Seth. Perhaps the shame was still too great. Regardless, there is no mention of walking with God beyond what we are told happened in Eden.

We do see this interesting development in today's text.

At that time people began to call on the name of the LORD.

It sounds like prayer, doesn't it? It is difficult, if not impossible, to understand what has been lost when you never experienced that which has been lost. Let's consider prayer as an example. We can hear and read about the depths of a prior generation's experience of faith and prayer and the nearness of God, and assume we are enjoying the same thing—if only to a lesser degree. The danger of the assumption is exposed only when someone has the audacity to ask the unthinkable question: What if we aren't even close?

I grew up in a church and a community probably like many of you. I had a sense there must be more to faith than I was getting, yet I was surrounded by people who seemed quite contented to accept that what they were experiencing must be *it*. The only ones who can't be awakened are those who are sure they are already awake. Again, it is impossible to understand what has been lost when you never experienced that which was lost.

It reminds me of those haunting words from the opening monologue of the movie *The Lord of the Rings: The Fellowship of the Ring:* "Much that once was is no longer, for none now live who remember it."

Something happened in that first generation of grandchildren that had not happened before. The Bible describes it as follows: *At that time people began to call on the name of the Lᴏʀᴅ.*

Did someone tell them the story of Eden and of a God who once walked with their grandparents in the garden in the cool of the day? Nostalgia for bygone days produces sentiment but rarely any noteworthy movement. It takes something approaching neediness or holy discontent before someone will call on the name of the Lord.

This is the seduction of liturgy. Liturgy attempts to capture the memory but it cannot carry the movement. Entire generations can be lulled to sleep while reciting the Lord's Prayer. Saying prayers, no matter how powerful the words, can often only amount to the motions. It takes someone digging beneath the water table of their own surface-level needs to get down to the deeper thirst where they finally call on the name of the Lord. This is where going through the motions breaks down and awakening to the movement breaks out.

And let's be clear. To call on the name of the Lord is a step in the right direction, but it does not yet even approximate what it means to walk with God. Said another way, to call on the name of the Lord is the beginning of a prayer life, but to walk with God is of another order—it means a life of prayer.

The seeds of awakening go into the ground when a generation begins to call on the name of the Lord. The fruit of awakening appears when a generation rises to walk with God.

The Prayer

Lord Jesus, you are right here, right now. I confess my own tendency to think that I have gotten what there is to get, when I know that there is more of you than I can ever comprehend. Put me more in touch with my need of you that I might more readily call on your name. Even more, I need you to take me by the hand and walk with me into a way of life I do not yet know. Right here, Jesus. Right now, Jesus. Amen.

The Questions

- What do you think of this distinction between the motions of faith and prayer and the movement of faith and prayer?
- When did your neediness or holy discontent reach a level where you began to really call on the name of the Lord?
- Reflect on how you understand the difference between a prayer life and a life of prayer.

The First Sermon I Ever Preached. The Text May Surprise You

15

GENESIS 5:21–24 | When Enoch had lived 65 years, he became the father of Methuselah. After he became the father of Methuselah, Enoch walked faithfully with God 300 years and had other sons and daughters. Altogether, Enoch lived a total of 365 years. Enoch walked faithfully with God; then he was no more, because God took him away.

Consider This

I remember it like it was yesterday. There I stood in the pulpit of the First United Methodist Church of Dumas, Arkansas, staring out on the faithful saints, many of whom expected that I would one day become the president of the United States. I sat in those pews for twenty-something years, never imagining I would stand in the pulpit to preach the Word of God. My chosen text for the only inaugural address I would ever give was Genesis 5:24.

Enoch walked faithfully with God; then he was no more, because God took him away.

I remember being won over by this obscure character who, in the midst of mindless genealogical rehearsals, gets a massive high-five from God. There's Adam, Seth, Enosh, Kenan, Mahalalel, Jared, Methuselah, Lamech, Noah, Shem, Ham, and Japheth.

Tucked in there between Jared and Methuselah we meet the man of the hour, Enoch. Of all the people singled out for mention, not to mention the unnamed multitudes, Enoch gets a special commendation.

Enoch walked faithfully with God; then he was no more, because God took him away.

Why this text for my first sermon ever? I can only speculate all these years later.

I think my life to that point had been more about running the world's race than walking with God. I think I was ready to stop running a race for yet another trophy that would not matter in the end. Honestly, I think those were the days when I stopped running that race and started walking with God. Sure, I called on the name of the Lord before then, but it was more calling on God to bless my plans and help me win my race. Walking with God meant letting go of the never-ending résumé-building quest to make a name for myself. Maybe I got a glimpse of the fleeting nature of life and caught a vision of the future when I would be no more. I wondered what, if anything, would be said of me, and what word would endure about the life I lived. I knew that I knew Jesus. I think I feared arriving at the end filled with regret about missing the point of my life. Somehow I knew back then the point of my life on earth would only be found by walking with God. I still believe this.

One more observation. Some of you reading may be thinking, *I wish I had discovered this much earlier in my life. How different or how much richer my life might have been.* Take heart, Enoch didn't start walking with God until he was sixty-five years old.

As said earlier in this series, walking with God means graduating from a life where prayer constitutes the punctuation marks, to a life where prayer is the prose and, finally, the poetry. It is to shift from a prayer life to a life of prayer.

Enoch walked faithfully with God; then he was no more, because God took him away.

I hear you. "Enough of the fluffy language," you say. "How does one make such a transition?"

It starts by seeing the difference—between a prayer life and a life of prayer; between calling on the name of the Lord and walking with God. It grows not by ratcheting up the discipline but by reorienting our desires. In truth, we will walk with God to the extent we desire this more than anything else. I like the way Mother Teresa made this point. Let's give her the last word today: "If you do not pray, your words will have no power; your life will have no power. Prayer enlarges the heart until it is capable of containing God's gift of himself."

The Prayer

Lord Jesus, you are right here, right now. I'm weary of trying to grow my prayer life and constantly feeling like I'm not really growing. I am ready to grow by order of magnitude rather than incremental degrees. I want to walk with you. I want this to be the core integrating desire of my life. Lead me. Right here, Jesus. Right now, Jesus. Amen.

The Questions

- How do you evaluate where you are at this point in your life? Prayer life or life of prayer?
- Who comes to mind in your own life and history as a person who walked with God?
- What characteristics stand out to you about a person who walks with God?

Why I Don't Believe Most People Are Good

16

GENESIS 6:5–9 | The Lᴏʀᴅ saw how great the wickedness of the human race had become on the earth, and that every inclination of the thoughts of the human heart was only evil all the time. The Lᴏʀᴅ regretted that he had made human beings on the earth, and his heart was deeply troubled. So the Lᴏʀᴅ said, "I will wipe from the face of the earth the human race I have created—and with them the animals, the birds and the creatures that move along the ground—for I regret that I have made them." But Noah found favor in the eyes of the Lᴏʀᴅ.

This is the account of Noah and his family.

Noah was a righteous man, blameless among the people of his time, and he walked faithfully with God.

Consider This

They say country music is three chords and the truth. I recently heard a song on the radio causing me to question this adage. It's called "Most People Are Good."

To that I say, "Tell Jesus." Remember that time the young ruler greeted Jesus as, "Good teacher?" Remember how Jesus responded? "Why do you call me good? . . . No one is good—except God alone" (Mark 10:17–18). Somehow I can't hear Jesus singing the tune "Most People Are Good" from the cross.

So are most people bad? People are not good because they do good. Nor are they bad because they do bad. Here's how I would put it. All people are sinners, which means all people are corrupt. We are broken. We are capable of doing really good things and unthinkably bad things. The problem with unhealed broken sinners is the way we break others. This can go unchecked, passed down, and compounded from generation to generation. That's what we find in Genesis 6.

The Lord saw how great the wickedness of the human race had become on the earth, and that every inclination of the thoughts of the human heart was only evil all the time.

Yep, that's what they were dealing with: multigenerational sin and brokenness, unchecked, unhealed, passed down, and compounded. It was bad. The chaos had returned with a vengeance. Into this dark chapter, we meet Noah and his family.

Noah was a righteous man, blameless among the people of his time, and he walked faithfully with God.

How does one family manage to go against the grain of the whole world? What was different about Noah and his family? He walked with God. Noah didn't walk with God because he was somehow different than or more righteous than anyone else. Noah was righteous because he walked with God.

We get so easily deceived at this point. We think walking with God comes down to our efforts to be righteous—to be different from *those* people. We think our so-called good choices make us good. They don't. This is called self-righteousness and, honestly, it is just as bad as unrighteousness—maybe even worse. It is walking with God that makes us righteous. Righteousness is not measured by right behavior, but by a much deeper wellness at the core of our soul. Righteousness comes not from being right *for* God, but from being right *with* God. True righteousness only comes from God.

And I must share some good news at this point: "For Christ also suffered once for sins, the righteous for the unrighteous, to bring you to God. He was put to death in the body but made alive in the Spirit" (1 Peter 3:18).

"This is how God showed his love among us: He sent his one and only Son into the world that we might live through him. This is love: not that we loved God, but that he loved us and sent his Son as an atoning sacrifice for our sins" (1 John 4:9–10).

Walking with God means learning to walk in the mercy of Jesus Christ. One of my everyday idiosyncratic discipleship practices is to say a form of the Jesus Prayer every time I walk up or down a flight of stairs. With each step I say the next word of the prayer, "Lord Jesus Christ, have mercy on me, a sinner."[5]

Over the years, it has become a tangible way of walking with God. Interestingly, the more I walk with God, and the nearer I find myself to God, the more mercy I need. It would seem to be just the opposite. It's not. As I have grown in my walk, I have added to the prayer (which means I need about three flights of stairs to say the whole thing). It goes like this:

Lord Jesus Christ, have mercy on me, a sinner.

Lord Jesus Christ, have mercy on me, a son.

Lord Jesus Christ, have mercy on me, a saint.

---

5 I got this particular prayer from a book called *The Way of the Pilgrim*.

I find myself living in some dimension of all three at any given point. I call them my "walking with God on the stairs" prayers. And I commend the practice to you. Let me know how it goes.

Noah was a righteous man, blameless among the people of his time, and he walked faithfully with God.

The Prayer

Lord Jesus, you are right here, right now. Thank you for telling us the truth, that no one is good but God. Save me from the prideful deception of thinking I am good based on what goodness I do. Save me from the shame-filled deception that I am bad based on the bad things I do. Awaken me to the grace of Jesus Christ, who makes me righteous and who fits me to walk with God. Right here, Jesus. Right now, Jesus. Amen.

The Questions

- What do you think about human nature? Are people basically good?
- How do you understand the nature of the gospel? Making good people better or bringing dead people to life?
- What do you make of this idea that we need more mercy to walk with God as a saint than we need as a sinner?

The Antithesis of Prayer 17

GENESIS 11:1–9 | Now the whole world had one language and a common speech. As people moved eastward, they found a plain in Shinar and settled there.

They said to each other, "Come, let's make bricks and bake them thoroughly." They used brick instead of stone, and tar for mortar. Then they said, "Come, let us build ourselves a city, with a tower that reaches to the heavens, so that we may make a name for ourselves; otherwise we will be scattered over the face of the whole earth."

But the Lord came down to see the city and the tower the people were building. The Lord said, "If as one people speaking the same language they have begun to do this, then nothing they plan to do will be impossible for them. Come, let us go down and confuse their language so they will not understand each other."

So the Lord scattered them from there over all the earth, and they stopped building the city. That is why it was called Babel—because there the Lord confused the language of the whole world. From there the Lord scattered them over the face of the whole earth.

Consider This

Some years back I saw a story about an ad campaign running on subways in one of America's major cities. The signs said, "Prayer won't cure AIDS. Research will."

It feels like such a brazen swing at God. That's the spirit of Babel.

God has given the human race enormous power. Though their power does not come within a million miles of the power of God, they somehow believe they can rival God.

Then they said, "Come, let us build ourselves a city, with a tower that reaches to the heavens, so that we may make a name for ourselves."

This story we know as the Tower of Babel reveals the antithesis of prayer, which is conspiring together against God to build our own kingdom. It is making agreements with one another to the end that "our kingdom come and our will be done, in heaven as it is on earth."

Whether we mean to or not, when we leave God out of the equation, we start building our own tower. This happens in the world on a grand scale every day. As the followers of Jesus, we don't feel so susceptible to doing such a thing.

I wonder though, what does God think when we hatch our plans and develop our blueprints first and only ask God to get on board when we run into challenges?

I've learned over the years in writing the Daily Text to ask for help early—like before I write the first word. It works so much better than asking him to bail out my half-baked idea midway through. In fact, I think I'll leave it there for now. Anything else today could well be more Babel.

And to be sure, prayer won't cure AIDS; neither will research. Only God can do that.

The Prayer

Lord Jesus, you are right here, right now. You see the end of all things even before the beginning. Forgive me for launching into my plans without inquiring of you. Train me to walk with you in such a way that I only do what I see you doing and only say what I hear you saying. I'm weary of my own ways. I need Holy Spirit instincts. Right here, Jesus. Right now, Jesus. Amen.

The Questions

- What is it about human nature that makes us want to launch out with our own agenda to do things for God and then ask him to bless them?
- What keeps us from beginning with God?
- What would it look like to walk with God in such a way that our agenda flows out of relationship? What does a step in that direction look like for you?

Why Walking with God Means Traveling without an Itinerary

18

GENESIS 12:1–5 | The LORD had said to Abram, "Go from your country, your people and your father's household to the land I will show you. "I will make you into a great nation, and I will bless you; I will make your name great, and you will be a blessing. I will bless those who bless you, and whoever curses you I will curse; and all peoples on earth will be blessed through you."

So Abram went, as the Lᴏʀᴅ had told him; and Lot went with him. Abram was seventy-five years old when he set out from Harran. He took his wife Sarai, his nephew Lot, all the possessions they had accumulated and the people they had acquired in Harran, and they set out for the land of Canaan, and they arrived there.

Consider This

Walking with God is far from a romantic adventure. It is to leave home on a trip without knowing the destination. In other words, when we walk with the Lord we gain the great gift of God's presence but we lose any sense of itinerary. Did you catch that in today's text?

The Lᴏʀᴅ had said to Abram, "Go from your country, your people and your father's household to the land I will show you."

God didn't tell Abram where he was going—only to go. God began with a man and a woman in a flourishing garden. After eleven chapters of catastrophic failure, God begins again, only this time he chooses not to begin with flourishing but barrenness. God begins again with a man and woman of advanced years and no family.

This time, God does not speak words of creation, but of the promise of new creation, again with unbridled flourishing.

"I will make you into a great nation, and I will bless you; I will make your name great, and you will be a blessing. I will bless those who bless you, and whoever curses you I will curse; and all peoples on earth will be blessed through you."

Then we get the three words that start Genesis all over again: *So Abram went.*

So why does this text qualify for our Daily Text series on prayer? Abram shows us something utterly essential for anyone who aspires to walk with God in a life of prayer. I call it preemptive obedience. In making the decision to trust God's promise, Abram decided in advance he would obey all of God's instructions to come. The sure sign of trust in a promise is obedience to a plan you don't get to see in advance. Yes, walking with God means traveling without an itinerary.

I'm not going to lie. This is not easy. It will surface every ounce of insecurity and fear within us. Trust, obedience, prayer, faith—this is the curriculum. Obedience is to trust as faith is to prayer. These are massive concepts that cannot really be thought through—only walked out. These ideas dwell in the realm of poetry, better yet, song.

Back in 1887 John Sammis penned lyrics to a hymn that captures these mind-bending ideas, "Trust and Obey." Let's give him the last word today.

> When we walk with the Lord
> In the light of His Word,
> What a glory He sheds on our way;
> While we do His good will,
> He abides with us still,
> And with all who will trust and obey.
>
> Trust and obey,
> For there's no other way

> To be happy in Jesus,
> But to trust and obey.

The Prayer

Lord Jesus, you are right here, right now. I love the idea that you have a plan for my life. I just want you to give it to me. Instead, you offer me yourself. I confess, I still want the itinerary. Teach me to trust and obey. Train my mind and heart with the grace of preemptive obedience. Right here, Jesus. Right now, Jesus. Amen.

The Questions

- Have you ever wondered how many people might have turned God down before he approached Abraham? Any thoughts about that?
- What makes it difficult for us to add preemptive obedience to our trust? What about you, in particular, makes it hard to trust and obey?
- Think about how readily you will trust your phone's GPS for directions to get somewhere. What if you could trust Jesus like that?

19 On Building Altars

GENESIS 12:6–8 | Abram traveled through the land as far as the site of the great tree of Moreh at Shechem. At that time the Canaanites were in the land. The Lord appeared to Abram and

RIGHT HERE. RIGHT NOW.

said, "To your offspring I will give this land." So he built an altar there to the Lord, who had appeared to him.

From there he went on toward the hills east of Bethel and pitched his tent, with Bethel on the west and Ai on the east. There he built an altar to the Lord and called on the name of the Lord.

Consider This

Abram traveled.

It seems obvious to say, but walking with God means movement. It means going from one place to another. It is not the travel of tourists following an itinerary, but of pilgrims following after God.

Sometimes the distance can be measured by actual miles. Often the geography traversed can only be measured in one's soul. Either way, when it comes to the movement of walking with God, the mile markers are altars.

An altar is a visible sign of an otherwise unseen reality. To make an altar to the Lord takes prayer from the invisible realm and transforms it into a visible reality. Altars create places in real time and space to mark progress in an otherwise unmeasurable journey. Abram did not know his destination. He only knew his God. In that sense, his God was his destination. Couldn't he have known that at home and topped it off with a good quiet time every morning? If God is the destination and God is with us, why do we ever need to go anywhere, right? This is the seductive place where our faith becomes domesticated and slowly slips from the movemental dynamic of our life to a spiritual spa.

Let's be clear, sometimes faith means physically going somewhere; other times not. Faith always means movement, because God is always on the move.

I can point to a series of altars in my past, critical turning points where I stopped to mark the action of God and my own surrendered responsiveness. I remember altars where I buried hurt and unforgiveness I had been carrying from the past. I remember altars where I burned written confessions of sin that had bound me. I remember altars where I laid face down on the ground with my arms extended outward in the shape of the cross. In each of those places I would name the Lord according to what he had done in my life.

The Prayer

Lord Jesus, you are right here, right now. There are so many times in the past when you have moved in my life and I have just moved on. I never marked the moment. Fill me with the grace to start marking your movements in my life. Right here, Jesus. Right now, Jesus. Amen.

The Questions

- Have you ever made an altar and commemorated the activity of God in your life?
- Why are altars important in biblical times? In today's times?
- What altar might you consider making in your life today?

The Difference between Loving God's Blessings and Loving God

20

GENESIS 15:1–8 | After this, the word of the Lord came to Abram in a vision: "Do not be afraid, Abram. I am your shield, your very great reward."

But Abram said, "Sovereign Lord, what can you give me since I remain childless and the one who will inherit my estate is Eliezer of Damascus?" And Abram said, "You have given me no children; so a servant in my household will be my heir."

Then the word of the Lord came to him: "This man will not be your heir, but a son who is your own flesh and blood will be your heir." He took him outside and said, "Look up at the sky and count the stars—if indeed you can count them." Then he said to him, "So shall your offspring be."

Abram believed the Lord, and he credited it to him as righteousness.

He also said to him, "I am the Lord, who brought you out of Ur of the Chaldeans to give you this land to take possession of it."

But Abram said, "Sovereign Lord, how can I know that I will gain possession of it?"

Consider This

By the time we get to chapter 15 of Genesis, the dangers, toils, and snares are starting to stack up.

To this point, Abram dealt with difficult family tensions with the gracious separation from Lot and company. They endured a famine that drove them to Egypt for refuge where Abram made the ill-advised decision to pass his wife off to Pharaoh as his sister. Along the way, Abram became very wealthy with many possessions and holdings. Meanwhile, Abram had to rescue his nephew Lot from a disaster and in the process met the famed Priest-King Melchizedek.

All of this to say, walking with God is no cakewalk. It is filled with trials, hardships, and difficulties. This is par for the course, whether one walks with God or not. So what's the benefit of walking with God, if it is not an easier way? We see part of it in today's text.

"Do not be afraid, Abram. I am your shield, your very great reward."

Remember how it began with Abram?

> I will make you into a great nation, and I will bless you; I will make your name great, and you will be a blessing. I will bless those who bless you, and whoever curses you I will curse; and all peoples on earth will be blessed through you. (Gen. 12:2–3)

We tend to follow after the call of God because of the promise of blessings. And those blessings come, but not without hardship and even suffering along with them. There comes a point on the journey in the walk with God where we discover the real blessing is the Lord himself: "*[I am] your very great reward.*"

Abram still had more questions. We all do. We all want to know, "Why this, Jesus, and why not that, and couldn't you have done something and why didn't you?" Meanwhile, through it all, he walks with us, from our first step through our worst falls. Somewhere along the way when we begin making that shift from a prayer life to a life of prayer we discover even the blessings pale in comparison to the One who blesses. After rehearsing his privileged and set-apart life, the apostle Paul captured it with these words:

> But whatever were gains to me I now consider loss for the sake of Christ. What is more, I consider everything a loss because of the surpassing worth of knowing Christ Jesus my Lord, for whose sake I have lost all things. I consider them garbage, that I may gain Christ. (Phil. 3:7–8)

Blessings come and go, as do trials and difficulties. Paul said it well when he said,

> I know what it is to be in need, and I know what it is to have plenty. I have learned the secret of being content in any and every situation, whether well fed or hungry, whether living in plenty or in want. I can do all this through him who gives me strength. (Phil. 4:12–13)

It is through the faith of those who walk with God that God reclaims the chaos, restores the broken, and establishes his kingdom, on earth as it is in heaven.

There's more to say about today's text, which we will pick up tomorrow. Let's give the slave-runner–turned-saint, John Newton, the last word today from stanza 3 of his celebrated hymn, "Amazing Grace": "Through many dangers toils and snares I have already come. 'Tis grace hath brought me safe thus far, and grace will lead me home."

The Prayer

Lord Jesus, you are right here, right now. I once thought life would be easier following you. I know better now. I do know that many things that seemed hard before have become sources of great blessing. I am ready to learn in a new way that you are the treasure. Take me to the place where knowing you is the greatest blessing. Right here, Jesus. Right now, Jesus. Amen.

The Questions

- Have you discovered that those who walk with God have as much, if not more, trials and difficulties than those who don't?
- Have you come to the place in your walk with God where you love God more than you love his blessings? Have you come to the place where you love God even without his blessings?
- What does it mean that the Lord is our very great reward? What other rewards might we have been hoping for?

Why the Gospel of Believing and Behaving Is Not the Gospel

21

GENESIS 15:5–8 | He took him outside and said, "Look up at the sky and count the stars—if indeed you can count them." Then he said to him, "So shall your offspring be."

Abram believed the LORD, and he credited it to him as righteousness.

He also said to him, "I am the LORD, who brought you out of Ur of the Chaldeans to give you this land to take possession of it."

But Abram said, "Sovereign LORD, how can I know that I will gain possession of it?"

Consider This

Abram had questions. We all do. To walk with God in a life of prayer, which means to walk by faith, is not the way of certainty. Neither is faith the way of uncertainty. Faith operates from another framework altogether—the framework of confident movement. It is why the way is found by walking— not sitting. We tend to crave measurable certainty before making a decision to act. In the realm of faith, the only way to gain certainty is to act first. Certainty becomes the fruit of exercised confidence. Our native mentality says, "I will

believe it when I see it." The mentality of faith says the opposite, "I will see it when I believe it."

Let's be clear about something. This is not believism or
faith in faith, as some have supposed. This is why faith is
not about praying harder or longer or somehow more effectively. The way of faith revealed in Scripture puts all the
emphasis not on the subject or even the verbiage of faith but
on faith's object. It's why Jesus would later say faith as small
as a mustard seed will do—because it's not the size of one's
faith that matters but the nature of one's God. This is why
biblical faith can be so laced with uncertainty and doubt.
Walking with God in a life of prayer is all about the progres-
sive exchanging of confidence in oneself for confidence in
one's God. Biblical faith is the movement from self-reliance
to reliance on God—Father, Son, and Holy Spirit.

We have lived through a period of history wherein faith
was assumed to be belief in the right things about God or
intellectual assent to a set of propositional truths. It's not that
the propositional truths are not true, it is that biblical faith
is of another order entirely. Biblical faith is not primarily an
exercise of believing truths about God. Faith is decisive risk-
taking movement and confident reliance on the God who is
himself the Way and the Truth and the Life.

That was the setup for today's most momentous text. In
yesterday's text, we saw Abram asking lots of questions of
this God with whom he had been walking. He wanted to
know how on earth he would be the father of a great nation
since he remained childless. He wanted to know how his

estate would remain in his family given he had no heir. He wanted to know how he would gain possession of the land that had been promised to him. It is in the midst of this seeming doubt and uncertainty that we got the following word, which unveiled for us perhaps the most core principle in all of Scripture: *Abram believed the LORD, and he credited it to him as righteousness.*

With all his questions, doubts, and uncertainties, when push came to shove, Abram kept walking with God. He looked past the promises to the Promise-Maker himself and he kept making decisive risk-taking movements. God has a name for such behavior; he calls it *righteousness*. What? I thought righteousness meant following the rules, crossing the t's and dotting the i's and all that. Righteousness does not come from following the rules but trusting the Ruler. Righteousness comes from following the Righteous One. Righteousness comes by faith.

We've been taught that the path to righteousness is believing and behaving. To be clear, there's nothing wrong with believing and behaving. It's just not the path to righteousness. The path to righteousness is risk-taking trust in Jesus. Let's give him the last word today. It makes sense that he would say, "Seek first his kingdom and his righteousness, and all these things will be given to you as well" (Matt. 6:33).

The Prayer

Lord Jesus, you are right here, right now. I love your promises, but I love you more. Following you is life and way and truth. Your righteousness is better than life. Your kingdom is better than the best. Free me from all that holds me back that I might seek you with all I am. Right here, Jesus. Right now, Jesus. Amen.

The Questions
- How did we come to understand righteousness primarily as believing and behaving? What went wrong?
- Have you struggled with a propositional faith rather than a real risk-taking faith? How did you break free?
- What role has doubt and uncertainty played in your walk with God?

22 A God Who Swears on His Life . . . for Us

GENESIS 15:9–21 | So the LORD said to him, "Bring me a heifer, a goat and a ram, each three years old, along with a dove and a young pigeon."

Abram brought all these to him, cut them in two and arranged the halves opposite each other; the birds, however, he did not cut in half. Then birds of prey came down on the carcasses, but Abram drove them away.

As the sun was setting, Abram fell into a deep sleep, and a thick and dreadful darkness came over him. Then the LORD said to him, "Know for certain that for four hundred years your descendants will be strangers in a country not their own and that they will be enslaved and mistreated there. But I will punish the nation they serve as slaves, and afterward they will come out with great possessions. You, however, will go to your ancestors in peace and be buried at a good old age. In the fourth generation your descendants will come back here, for the sin of the Amorites has not yet reached its full measure."

When the sun had set and darkness had fallen, a smoking firepot with a blazing torch appeared and passed between the pieces. On that day the Lord made a covenant with Abram and said, "To your descendants I give this land, from the Wadi of Egypt to the great river, the Euphrates—the land of the Kenites, Kenizzites, Kadmonites, Hittites, Perizzites, Rephaites, Amorites, Canaanites, Girgashites and Jebusites."

Consider This

Yesterday, I put it like this: "The way of faith revealed in Scripture puts all the emphasis not on the subject or even the verbiage of faith but on faith's object. It's why Jesus would later say faith as small as a mustard seed will do—because it's not the size of one's faith that matters but the nature of one's God."

Today's text reveals the extraordinary nature of the God of Abram, who is our God. In response to Abram's questions and concerns, God does something truly incredible. He "cuts" a covenant with Abram. The all-powerful Creator God entered into an agreement with the finite, fallen man, Abram, and bound himself to keep his promise.

I love the way my dear friend Sandra Richter puts it in her game-changing study of the Old Testament, *The Epic of Eden*:

> In other words, the Creator of the Cosmos, the Lord of the stars has descended to Abram's desert location to speak words of faith. He says to Abram, I swear to you on my life that I am going to bring this promise to pass. May what has happened to these animals happen to me if I break covenant with you.

This is the God with whom we walk, the one to whom we pray. Creation and covenant. Trust and obedience. Prayer and faith. These are the ways of walking with God.

Look again at the shape of God's Word. Yes, God will fulfill his promise.

"To your descendants I give this land,"

It will take time, though. And there will be hardship and suffering all along the way.

"Know for certain that for four hundred years your descendants will be strangers in a country not their own and that they will be enslaved and mistreated there."

There will be reprieve and restoration as well.

"But I will punish the nation they serve as slaves, and afterward they will come out with great possessions."

Creation is God's intention. Covenant is God's direction. We navigate this walk with God by trust and obedience, prayer and faith, intention and attention, and yes, through many dangers, toils, and snares, and over a long stretch of time.

This is a multigenerational project. We have harvested where we have not sown, and we must now sow where we will not harvest. We must take care not to get sidetracked with the distractions of false gospels that would domesticate our faith.

Consider now the new covenant made with us by Jesus Christ. His very body took the place of the slain sacrifices in the covenant with Abram. Consider the implications of praying as he instructed us, in his name.

The Prayer

Lord Jesus, you are right here, right now. Thank you for calling us to be your disciples and for opening our eyes to this way of walking with you. We need more understanding and yet we sense you nudging us toward more faith. Shake us from our complacency. Awaken us to full participation in your kingdom. Right here, Jesus. Right now, Jesus. Amen.

The Questions

- What observations do you make about the nature of the God of Abram from the covenant God made with him?
- So if God knows about the four hundred years of slavery in Egypt, why not stop it? How do you deal with this?
- How does this help your understanding of faith being more about the nature of God than the strength or quality of your faith?

23 Travelogue: Recapping the Journey So Far

PSALM 110:1 | The Lord says to my lord: "Sit at my right hand until I make your enemies a footstool for your feet."

JOHN 15:7 ESV | "If you abide in me, and my words abide in you, ask whatever you wish, and it will be done for you."

EPHESIANS 6:18 | And pray in the Spirit on all occasions with all kinds of prayers and requests. With this in mind, be alert and always keep on praying for all the Lord's people.

Consider This

We've come quite a ways so far. Let's take a strategic look back and recount some of the ground we've covered.

From "Right Here. Right Now."

This is perhaps the first and most important teaching on prayer. We aren't sending our prayers "up there somewhere." We are speaking directly and immediately to the risen Son of God. Though unseen to the naked eye, he is right here, right now. Jesus is not with us in the sense that someone who can't come to our birthday party says they will be with us "in spirit." Jesus is not with us in spirit, but in person—in the power of the Holy Spirit.

From "The War of Prayer"

Prayer means many things to many people. Biblically speaking, prayer means war. Prayer means advance. Prayer means recovering what has been lost and taking back what has been stolen.

From "On the Necessity of Becoming a Beginner Again"

The Christian vision of prayer is not empty-handed scarcity but overflowing fruit-full-ness. James said we have not because we ask not or we ask with wrong motives (James 4:2–3). This is why the Word of God is so central to prayer. Jesus is not a wish genie but a prayer trainer.

From "In the Beginning: Prayer"

The biblical foundation for prayer begins neither with preexistent nothingness nor with broken everything. Our whole understanding and practice of prayer must begin with the beginning—Genesis 1:1. It means prayer begins with faith. Now, by *faith*, I don't mean to say the activity of human belief, but the reality of divine action. Faith is the willful decision of a community of people to live the totality of their existence in the light of God and in the world of God's making.

From "The Three Most Powerful Words of Prayer"

Prayer, or speaking like God speaks, begins with incorporating these three words into our praying vocabulary: "Let there be . . ."

The world around us desperately needs people with the audacity to speak like God speaks—to speak words in the power of the Spirit into the formless, empty, dark, and deep situations. The world needs the followers of Jesus to become schooled and skilled with the creative speech of prayer.

From "Why Prayer Doesn't Work and Who Does"

Sometimes God moves mountains in an unmistakably sovereign way. More often, he moves us, by the strength of his Spirit, to move all the old furniture out of the chaotic storage room. Sometimes a word will get it done. Other times to that word we must add rolling up our sleeves. It's all God, though. And all good.

From "The True Way of Prayer Is Claim It and Name It"

There's a difference between saying prayers and praying. Saying prayers can train us for praying, but praying requires more than this. It requires the long, slow cultivation of a memory steeped in Scripture, an attentiveness anchored in the embodied human-ness of Jesus (which is our humanity), and an imagination fired by the Holy Spirit and imbued with all the possibilities of the kingdom of heaven.

From "Why Prayer Does Not Move God and What Does"

To tell another person, "I'll be praying for you," is a serious thing. It is not sitting passively and sympathetically on the outside, speaking words to God on their behalf. Rather, it means something more like, "I will stand with Jesus for you in the midst of the chaos." Real praying is not human-inspired sympathy but Spirit-empowered empathy.

From "Why Prayer Is Not the Solution to Our Problem"

To be sure, we live as fallen creatures in the midst of a fallen creation. We, however, are called to arise into the post-resurrection reality of our ascended Lord, where the new creation of the kingdom of heaven bursts at the seams to break in upon the broken order and renew the flourishing of all abundance.

From "How Prayer Leads Us into a Whole New World"

What if our most powerful and creative capacity as image-bearers of God is to speak like God speaks—to pray? Could this be what it means to rule like God rules—to walk with God in the ways of God, by the will of God, and in accordance with the Word of God? I am becoming convinced that this is what prayer means.

From "The Epic Fail of Eden"

Are we Genesis 1–2 people flourishing in abundance or are we Genesis 3 scarcity people? The resurrection and ascension of Jesus and the coming of the Holy Spirit doesn't all at once abolish the reality of Genesis 3; however, it opens a new and living way of prayer anchored far more in the possibilities of Eden and the new creation than in the problems of exile.

From "On the Difference between a Prayer Life and a Life of Prayer"

To call on the name of the Lord is a step in the right direction, but it does not yet even approximate what it means to walk with God. Said another way, to call on the name of the Lord is the beginning of a prayer life, but to walk with God is of another order—it means a life of prayer.

The Prayer

Lord Jesus, you are right here, right now. You are the only one who can teach us to pray. And so we ask you to teach us to pray as you pray. In fact, draw us into a participation in your very prayer life. Then we will know. Then we will rise up into a whole new world. Right here, Jesus. Right now, Jesus. Amen.

The Questions

- What stands out in your remembrance and learning from the series so far?
- How do you find yourself most challenged?
- On what points do you find your thinking and practice most confirmed and encouraged?

24 Prayer as Divine Negotiation

GENESIS 18:22–26 | The men turned away and went toward Sodom, but Abraham remained standing before the LORD. Then

Abraham approached him and said: "Will you sweep away the righteous with the wicked? What if there are fifty righteous people in the city? Will you really sweep it away and not spare the place for the sake of the fifty righteous people in it? Far be it from you to do such a thing—to kill the righteous with the wicked, treating the righteous and the wicked alike. Far be it from you! Will not the Judge of all the earth do right?"

The Lord said, "If I find fifty righteous people in the city of Sodom, I will spare the whole place for their sake."

Consider This

There's a word for the kind of praying we see in today's text, I'm just not sure what it is. To call it "bold" seems tepid. If you've never read the rest of this text, please take the time to do so. Bottom line: Abraham turns prayer on its side and moves it into the realm of a negotiation. It strikes us as all at once audacious and borderline insanity.

Something tells me this pleased the Lord. Why? Abraham lays hold of Sodom in a very God-like way. This is what prayer designs to do—to cause us to risk overstepping our bounds that we might find the boundary and run right up to it. God can handle our bravery in his presence far better than our passive tendency to play it safe.

And there's a word to be said here about the nature and interplay of prayer and faith. As I look back on so much of my former prayer life, I think my praying was more an expression of my hope that this whole God thing was real. Faith is not hopefulness in the reality of something you can't see.

Faith is a determined movement on a decided reality. Prayer navigates the movement. Prayer is not a Hail Mary pass into the end zone as the game clock expires. Prayer is not a "when all else fails, try prayer" last-resort remedy.

Prayer is the normative zone of interactivity between God and human beings founded in covenantal relationship and forged from a dogged and insistent clinging to the character of God—even to the point of reminding God of who he is.

"Far be it from you to do such a thing—to kill the righteous with the wicked, treating the righteous and the wicked alike. Far be it from you! Will not the Judge of all the earth do right?"

Note what Abraham is not praying. He does not say, "If there are fifty righteous people in the city, *and* if it is your will, would you spare the city from destruction?" Abraham asserts the will of God, based on the revealed character of God—that God will not treat the righteous and the wicked alike. This is not prayer as presumption but prayer as participation.

Is it God's will to save and deliver and heal people? Yes. Does God always save and deliver and heal? No. Why? We can't know. Sometimes it takes four hundred years of hindsight to even begin to understand a larger plan with ten thousand contingencies and a thousand seeming contradictions.

The bigger truth of redemption is the way God can save without apparent deliverance or healing. In the process of winning a war stretching across all of time and space, millions of battles are seemingly lost. God searches for people who will concede none of them; those who will never give up, never give in, never back down, and never let go. Why? Because love never gives up, never gives in, never backs down, and never lets go. It's why the school of prayer is the school of divine love. Even in the face of abject failure, the love of God never fails. Behold the cross.

At the end of the day, God would have saved Sodom for the sake of ten righteous people, but they could not be found. Still, God saved Lot.

The Prayer

Lord Jesus, you are right here, right now. I grasp this at a certain level and still it doesn't show forth in everyday life enough. Awaken me to real faith, bold audacity, and holy love. Nudge me out of my comfort zone today—okay, shove me—for the sake of your great name. Right here, Jesus. Right now, Jesus. Amen.

The Questions

- What stands out to you about today's text and Abraham's negotiation with God?
- Have you ever reminded God of his character and nature as a part of your praying? Reflect on that.
- What would it look like for you to push past the normal safe boundaries of your way of praying and relating to God and others?

25 There's Something about a Tree . . .

GENESIS 21:32–34 | After the treaty had been made at Beersheba, Abimelek and Phicol the commander of his forces returned to the land of the Philistines. Abraham planted a tamarisk tree in Beersheba, and there he called on the name of the LORD, the Eternal God. And Abraham stayed in the land of the Philistines for a long time.

Consider This

My father had a nearly forty-year tenure as the teacher of the five-year-old's Sunday school class at the First United Methodist Church of Dumas, Arkansas. One of his class traditions in those early years was to plant a tree together on the church grounds. Those trees became long-standing, living reminders, flourishing markers of the fragile immovability of faith, growth, and relationship.

I will forever remember one of the great acts of clerical malfeasance when the pastor (at the time) decided that the first and tallest tree needed to be removed to make room for new landscaping on the church property. I remember it like an untimely death as it has become something of a parable in my memory concerning the incredulity of the church of our time.

Something about a commemorative tree says something beyond the comprehension of so-called permanent memorials made of concrete and steel. If a picture is worth a thousand words, a tree must be worth millions.

Abraham planted a tamarisk tree in Beersheba . . .

So often in Scripture, we see our forebears making altars or stacking stones as markers of the Lord's mighty acts of salvation and grace. It strikes me that these are meant to point backward, causing reflective remembrance on God's mighty acts. A tree, on the other hand, means to point us forward into the generative possibilities of the future. A tree, planted in the way Abraham planted this tamarisk tree, is more than symbolic. It is a sign. A sign is a symbol that does more than stand for a deeper meaning. It participates in the meaning.

. . . and there he called on the name of the LORD, the Eternal God.

In other words, the tree not only symbolizes the prayer, in a far deeper and mysterious way, the tree *is* the prayer. The roots grow deep. The trunk grows upward and imperceptibly outward. The branches and leaves grow outward with abundant flourishing bearing both flower and fruit and, finally, seed.

Abraham lived in a land promised him by God and yet as a stranger. The ancient sign of a tree bridges the distance between the already-and-not-yet dimensions of faith and future, between earth and sky, history and eternity, loss and reward, even death and resurrection.

I want you to pray about planting a tree in the coming season of your own life. The Lord is awakening new things in your life and faith and bringing them together around you. It needs to be signed and sealed and marked in a tangible fashion. Perhaps we will do it in some measure together at the close of this series on prayer. Let's start praying about it now.

The Prayer

Lord Jesus, you are right here, right now. You teach us through trees, from Eden to the fig tree to the cross itself. May I learn from your life the ways of your Spirit, who would make me like a tree planted by streams of water that yields its fruit in season and whose leaves do not wither. Lead me into the only true prosperity, which is your kingdom—on earth as it is in heaven. Right here, Jesus. Right now, Jesus. Amen.

The Questions

- We all have tree stories. Consider sharing yours with your band or in our Facebook group or with your family around the table today.
- What biblical tree stories were brought to mind as you read today's text?
- What can be learned about the mystery of prayer in and through them?

26 Have You Learned the Prayer of Abandon?

GENESIS 22:1–5 | Some time later God tested Abraham. He said to him, "Abraham!"

"Here I am," he replied.

Then God said, "Take your son, your only son, whom you love—Isaac—and go to the region of Moriah. Sacrifice him there as a burnt offering on a mountain I will show you."

Early the next morning Abraham got up and loaded his donkey. He took with him two of his servants and his son Isaac. When he had cut enough wood for the burnt offering, he set out for the place God had told him about. On the third day Abraham looked up and saw the place in the distance. He said to his servants, "Stay here with the donkey while I and the boy go over there. We will worship and then we will come back to you."

Consider This

Remember those school days when they used to call the roll every morning? It was the official way for the school to find out who was present and who was absent. Remember the standard answer?

Teacher: John David Walt?

Here!

Sure, there were always those kids who had to say, "present," in order to be different. I won't say anything more about *those* kids because there are undoubtedly some of them reading along. I remember doing it a time or two myself.

Wouldn't it have been amazing if some kid along the way had answered the roll with, "Here I am!"? I wish I had thought of that.

There is something to publicly identifying oneself as "here."

There is a sense in which I believe Jesus calls our names every morning. To speak aloud the words, "Here I am," could become a significant practice of prayerful mindfulness to become conscience of the right here, right now presence of Jesus.

That's hardly the point of this most shocking biblical text. This text is a test of trust. I have mostly thought of it as a test of whether Abraham would trust God. I see it differently now. I think it is a test of whether God could trust Abraham.

In my judgment, God never intended Abraham to sacrifice his son, Isaac. After all, the story begins by telling us this was a test. Nor did Abraham ever intend to go through with it.

He said to his servants, "Stay here with the donkey while I and the boy go over there. We will worship and then we will come back to you."

It strikes me as a game of divine chicken. Who would flinch? In the end, it was God who flinched.

Isaac was the long-awaited answer to Abraham and Sarah's prayers. Abraham proved his faith was not founded in God's answer but in God himself. A life of prayer is built on trust. The trust, however, is not in the answer but in God.

It reminds me of the story of Shadrach, Meshach, and Abednego (or as Veggie Tales dubbed them, "Rack, Shack, and Benny"). Because they refused to worship Nebuchadnezzar's idolatrous image, he threatened to throw them into the fiery furnace. Their response is stellar:

> Shadrach, Meshach, and Abednego answered and said to the king, "O Nebuchadnezzar, we have no need to answer you in this matter. If this be so, our God whom

we serve is able to deliver us from the burning fiery furnace, and he will deliver us out of your hand, O king." (Dan. 3:16–17 ESV)

The next bit is epic—the stuff of legend: "But if not, be it known to you, O king, that we will not serve your gods or worship the golden image that you have set up" (Dan. 3:18 ESV).

A friend of mine, who against all odds remains a quite eligible bachelorette, recently had these three words inscribed in permanent ink on the inside of her wrist: "But if not." This is the mark of a true believer. It's not about placing our hope in the answer to our prayers, but the wholesale, full-scale abandonment of our lives to the One who is himself the answer—come what may. These are the ones whom God trusts.

So many of us are praying for and about so many things—good things. We want a soulmate or a child or a job or healing or deliverance or this or that blessing. Jesus wants to bless us with the desires of our heart. The greater glory is that he might become the desire our heart.

These three little words, "But if not." Let's call them the prayer of holy abandon.

The Prayer

Lord Jesus, you are right here, right now. We want so much from you. What we most want, though, is to come to the place where we want you more than your blessings. Teach me this "But if not" way of trust. I will not find it on my own. Right here, Jesus. Right now, Jesus. Amen.

The Questions

- Are you ready for the practice of sanctified imagination of answering the roll call of Jesus in the morning? "Here I am!" Try it and note the effect it has on your awareness and praying.
- Do you tend to put your trust and hope in the answer to your prayer or are you learning to place your trust and hope in God, regardless of the answer?
- What do you think of this "But if not" prayer? Would you be willing to add those words to the end of your normal way of praying? Note the effect on your faith.

27 Prayer Means Jesus Takes the Wheel

GENESIS 24:12–14 | Then he prayed, "Lᴏʀᴅ, God of my master Abraham, make me successful today, and show kindness to my master Abraham. See, I am standing beside this spring, and the daughters of the townspeople are coming out to draw water. May it be that when I say to a young woman, 'Please let down your jar that I may have a drink,' and she says, 'Drink, and I'll water your camels too'—let her be the one you have chosen for your servant Isaac. By this I will know that you have shown kindness to my master."

Consider This

Today's text jumps us forward a stretch from yesterday's incident of the near-sacrifice of Isaac. While Isaac no doubt continued to recover from the most horrifying event of his life, Abraham sent a servant on a mission to find him a wife. It was a high-pressure situation, requiring the servant to swear a rather awkward yet serious oath to Abraham.

The servant had a job to do and he wanted to do it well. He knew he needed help, so he made it a matter of prayer. Let's examine the prayer.

Then he prayed, "Lᴏʀᴅ, God of my master Abraham, make me successful today, and show kindness to my master Abraham."

Here's where the prayer gets pretty interesting.

"See, I am standing beside this spring, and the daughters of the townspeople are coming out to draw water. May it be that when I say to a young woman, 'Please let down your jar that I may have a drink,' and she says, 'Drink, and I'll water your camels too'—let her be the one you have chosen for your servant Isaac."

This servant had no control over the situation, yet he dared to visualize a quite specific outcome. It was not a miracle or some kind of sign or supernatural wonder he requested. Neither is it a random kind of confirmation. The servant was looking for a certain kind of extraordinary response that would perhaps signify an extraordinary kind of person.

It is speculative to suggest this, but I wonder if the servant knew what he would pray when he opened his mouth. Often when I pray I enter into a zone of interaction with God much like I enter a conversation with another person. In a conversation with someone I have a sense of what we will talk about but I don't know exactly what I am going to say. It's like that when I pray. I might begin by praying in a certain way, but once I'm into it I find myself thinking and saying things I never imagined I would say. It's because prayer takes me out of the driver's seat and allows Jesus to take the wheel.

In my experience, the Holy Spirit shapes my prayers as I pray. I'm speculating, but I think this is what happened that day as Abraham's servant prayed. In the act of praying he was led in how to pray.

Prayer creates a dynamic context for revelation in real time. It opens up a space for the working of the Holy Spirit to guide our understanding and discernment in ways they would not have gone otherwise. The letter to the Hebrews gets at what I am trying to convey:

> Therefore, brothers and sisters, since we have confidence to enter the Most Holy Place by the blood of Jesus, by a new and living way opened for us through the curtain, that is, his body, and since we have a great priest over the house of God, let us draw near to God with a sincere heart and with the full assurance that faith brings. (Heb. 10:19–22)

Prayer means confident movement into the Most Holy Place in this new and living way where new things can happen. More on this later as we enter the New Testament section of our study on prayer.

Most days we find ourselves in pressure-filled situations. We are out of our depth, beyond our resources, or up a creek without a paddle. We don't know what to do. Too often, we turn inward and dwell on our anxiety, turning it over in our mind, and because we feel desperate before God we consider ourselves praying. What if we could walk into a new room, open up a new kind of conversation with God, and allow Jesus to take the wheel for a bit? He's a great driver.

The Prayer

Lord Jesus, you are right here, right now. So often my prayer life is flat and even rote. It is like I am on the outside looking in. You are the new and living way. Open my mind and heart to enter into your life of prayer. By your Spirit, usher me into the inside where I can see out clearly. Right here, Jesus. Right now, Jesus. Amen.

The Questions

- What do you think of this speculation I am making about the servant's prayer that day?
- How do you relate to this idea of the Holy Spirit shaping our prayers as we pray—leading us in directions we would not have otherwise gone?
- Do you remember a time when prayer came alive to you in a new and living way? What was that like?

28 On Last Year's Branches and This Year's Fruit

GENESIS 25:21–23 | Isaac prayed to the LORD on behalf of his wife, because she was childless. The LORD answered his prayer, and his wife Rebekah became pregnant. The babies jostled each other within her, and she said, "Why is this happening to me?" So she went to inquire of the LORD.

The LORD said to her, "Two nations are in your womb, and two peoples from within you will be separated; one people will be stronger than the other, and the older will serve the younger."

Consider This

Most everyone believes in prayer, salutes the practice, and generally supports the idea. And truth be told, at one point or another, everyone does pray. In the United States, we still live in the wake of Christendom, and most people over thirty can recite the Lord's Prayer.

Becoming a person or a people of prayer—those who walk with God in a life of prayer—is another thing entirely. The real biblical vision of prayer has been obscured by the overwhelming tide of casual prayer; the fruit of a church who believes in God but does not follow Jesus.

We see something of the biblical vision in today's text. Isaac and Rebekah could not conceive a child. Welcome to the family of God, right? Just because God willed for Abraham to be the father of a great nation did not mean it would come easy. We are prone to believe that if God wills a thing, it will come easy. Scripture seems to prove just the opposite. The more God wills for a thing to happen, the greater the opposition and difficulty. God's will cannot be thwarted, but it can be severely taxed.

Today's text gives us a glimpse into the normative, non-casual life of prayer carried out by Isaac and Rebekah. Isaac prayed to the Lord on behalf of his wife, because she was childless. Isaac's prayers were answered and we move into difficulties in the pregnancy. Something disturbing was going on in Rebekah's womb. We would turn to the ultrasound scanner. Rebekah, we are told, "went to inquire of the LORD." Note how the first impulse and immediate response was to seek the Lord in prayer. They did not turn first to human invention and innovation. They began by seeking divine intervention.

Prayer will either be our navigational operating system or the window dressing of an otherwise nominal faith. As much as we want to believe in a comfortably reasonable in-between space, I'm sorry to say it does not exist. Prayer will be consuming or it will be casual—everything or nothing. Our salutes and stated belief in prayer count for nothing. I say these things not to shame or condemn, but to awaken.

In my own life, I have lived through long periods of time where prayer was my navigational system only to let it slowly slip away into casual nothingness in other seasons. Instead of a piercing self-honesty, I opted for the sloppy self-deception of self-assurance that last season's efforts would somehow carry over into this season's requirements. It doesn't work that way.

I will forever remember a line from a sermon I heard twenty-five years ago by a great man of God and leader of the church, Dr. David Gyertson. He was preaching on my favorite biblical text, John 15, and while referencing the words in verses 2–4 on pruning, he said, "You will never get this year's fruit off of last year's branches."

If I'm honest, and God knows I want to be, I need to proffer a confession. In 1990, I experienced a profound awakening to the presence and power of God. Along with this came the gift of a protracted season of intensive prayer. It was comprehensive and consuming, and those branches produced an enormous amount of fruit in my life and work.

As I reflect on it, I think I have attempted to harvest fruit from those branches ever since. I never ceased praying, but I believe my prayer life has receded in those intervening decades. I think the problem is that I have aspired to get back to that place. In the life of the indwelling Holy Spirit, there is no going back to the glory days of a bygone era, only pressing forward.

It is being revealed to me even now that the time has come to awaken again, to a new gift of prayer in a new season of life and work. Something tells me a pruning is long overdue in my life. The old branches are dead and rotten and must be cast down so new growth can appear. This new growth will be new, unfamiliar, and maybe even uncomfortable. My present norms, forms, and methods of prayer (i.e., the old wineskins) cannot hold the new wine the Spirit desires to pour forth (see Matthew 9:17; Mark 2:22; Luke 5:37–39).

I will stop there before I mix in yet another metaphor; however, I believe this word may not only be for myself but others. My sense is there is a word of prophecy here for perhaps a few others or maybe for many.

The Prayer

Lord Jesus, you are right here, right now. Thank you for always telling me the truth and, further, for telling me that the truth will set me free. Give me the gift of gut-level honesty about where I am and have been, yes, about sin, but more about casual faith. And open my eyes to the new thing you want to do. Right here, Jesus. Right now, Jesus. Amen.

The Questions

- Try this analogy from the tech world: Is prayer in your life more like an app on your phone or is it the whole operating system?
- Have you experienced periods of great awakening in your life to the things of God accompanied by surges in your life of prayer? Have those times, despite their blessings, ever been a hindrance in going forward to new and greater things?
- Is your vision of future possibilities of personal or even large-scale awakening limited by what has happened in the past? What might pruning look like in your life going

forward? Are you prepared to let go of what worked in the past and to go back to square one again?

29 The Day the House Entered Me

GENESIS 28:10–13, 16–17 | Jacob left Beersheba and set out for Harran. When he reached a certain place, he stopped for the night because the sun had set. Taking one of the stones there, he put it under his head and lay down to sleep. He had a dream in which he saw a stairway resting on the earth, with its top reaching to heaven, and the angels of God were ascending and descending on it. There above it stood the LORD, and he said: "I am the LORD, the God of your father Abraham and the God of Isaac. I will give you and your descendants the land on which you are lying. . . .

When Jacob awoke from his sleep, he thought, "Surely the LORD is in this place, and I was not aware of it." He was afraid and said, "How awesome is this place! This is none other than the house of God; this is the gate of heaven."

Consider This

When Jacob awoke from his sleep . . .

I will forever remember the night I awoke from my sleep. It was my second year of law school as I made my rounds across the campus of the Central United Methodist Church in

Fayetteville, Arkansas. Shake the doors. Turn off any lights. Ward off skate boarders. The usual church security guard fare. I just wanted to get it done quickly and get back to *Sports Center*. Little did I know, something would happen this night to change the course of my life.

I rounded the education building and made the turn to the temple complex (i.e., the sanctuary). I grasped the handle on the large front door and gave it a brisk pull, expecting the predictable rattling sound of the secured dead bolt. Instead, for the first time in my career, the door pulled open. I don't know why I didn't simply lock it up and resume my duties. I don't know why, but I decided to venture inside.

I walked down the center aisle of the majestic room, with its cavernous ceilings. As moonlight streamed in through the massive arched windows, and the sound of pure silence held the room, the impression of the following words began to rise up within me—as if to awaken my soul.

"My Father's house shall be called a house of prayer."

I spoke the words aloud.

"My Father's house shall be called a house of prayer."

I felt compelled to proceed down the aisle, straight up to the altar, where I knelt and began to speak aloud to God and everything changed. I'd sat in this church (and others like it), ten thousand times before. It was my Bethel moment.

"Surely the LORD is in this place, and I was not aware of it."

It was as though I had stepped inside the wardrobe and came out in Lewis's Narnia. I was no longer just in the house. The house had entered me.

"How awesome is this place! This is none other than the house of God; this is the gate of heaven."

All of this gins up a new and powerful obvious insight for me. It's not so much that the house of God is a house of prayer. Rather, the house of prayer is the house of God.

And the house of God cannot be built by human hands. The house of God is the people of God. It is me. It is you. It is us. The great and yet unrealized gift of Pentecost and the outpouring of the Holy Spirit is God does not dwell in temples built by human hands, but in his blood-bought image-bearers—the body of Christ.

This house of prayer, which is the house of God, is the place of God's activity, of the constancy of his ascending and descending, bringing heaven to earth and earth to heaven until the day of his return shall come when they can no longer be separated—for the glory of God will have covered the earth as the waters cover the sea.

We have gone to church all these years, and still do. It is long past time for our appointed Bethel moment, when we wake from our sleep with the soul-piercing epiphany: *Surely the Lord is in this place, and I was not aware of it.* And, of course, the "this place" I am referring to is my life and your life and our lives together. This will be the beginning of a great awakening.

The Prayer

Lord Jesus, you are right here, right now. You are not standing beside me but you are dwelling within me. Because of this, my life, my physical body, is your house. Forgive me for all the ways I have and continue to work against this; from my bodily habits to my life of prayer. I want to go with you fully, completely, unreservedly. Come, Holy Spirit, and align me with the kingdom purposes of the King of kings. Right here, Jesus. Right now, Jesus. Amen.

The Questions
- Have you had a Bethel moment before? Consider sharing it with us.
- How do you reflect on this reversal of phrase—the house of God is not a house of prayer—but the house of prayer is the house of God? More than semantics here?
- What do you think it will take for an awakening of this sort and magnitude to spread?

The Prayer of Groaning 30

EXODUS 2:23–25 | During that long period, the king of Egypt died. The Israelites groaned in their slavery and cried out, and their cry for help because of their slavery went up to God. God heard their groaning and he remembered his covenant with Abraham, with Isaac and with Jacob. So God looked on the Israelites and was concerned about them.

Consider This

During that long period . . .

We find ourselves in the story of Moses. Israel lived in the land of Egypt and after many years found themselves enslaved and oppressed under the power of the Pharaohs.

The law of sin and death, while utterly uncreative, operates with enormous sophistication and complexity. We have gone from a sky-scraping tower reaching to the heavens to a nation who enshrines its leaders as god incarnate. We have gone from a garden where God walks with his image-bearers in the cool of the day to a desert land where the god of the age, a.k.a. Pharaoh, asserts ownership over them, forcing them to build his kingdom.

That's what slavery is—when the image-bearers of the true God enter the service (voluntarily or involuntarily) of another kingdom under the control and influence of another (invariably false) god. These gods are all ultimately the same, ranging from Pharaoh to money to opioids. They all promise some form of Eden-like reality none of them can ultimately deliver.

What they ultimately deliver is groaning. Slavery always leads to groaning.

The Israelites groaned in their slavery and cried out, and their cry for help because of their slavery went up to God.

Why groaning? Groaning should not be confused with groveling. God doesn't look for groveling. Neither do I think it takes groaning to get God's attention. Groaning is the sign of the crystallized consolidation of our attention. And let's be honest: our attention needs to be crystallized and consolidated.

We like options and alternatives and multiple possible solutions for our desperate situations. So many so-called solutions are designed to avert our desperation. All the while, desperation is our solution. Desperation will either divide our attention among a multitude of possible solutions or it will consolidate our attention to a singular hope in God. The former looks like gritting our teeth and leads to anxiety; the latter looks like groaning and leads to peace.

Let me be clear. God's solutions can take all sorts of forms and shapes from medication to miraculous intervention. It's all in how we get there. We live in the self-deceived illusion of so many possible alternatives to God when God is the only alternative.

In Paul's letter to the church in Rome he tells us, "the Spirit himself intercedes for us through wordless groans" (Rom. 8:26). In fact, just prior to this, Paul says:

> We know that the whole creation has been groaning as in the pains of childbirth right up to the present time. Not only so, but we ourselves, who have the firstfruits of the Spirit, groan inwardly as we wait eagerly for our adoption to sonship, the redemption of our bodies. (Rom. 8:22–23)

It's a mistake to think of groaning as some kind of learned intensity in intercession or a particular expression of emotion in prayer. While those characteristics may or may not be present, the prayer of groaning is much more.

Dr. David Thomas, one of the key leaders in our work with Seedbed, recently spent the better part of a decade earning a PhD through researching and writing on this way of prayer and its historic connection with great awakenings. He calls it "travailing prayer." He points out how it is not something human desire or effort can produce. In a New Room address we published into a small booklet *To Sow for a Great Awakening* (part of our Seedlings series), David spoke of travail as:

> a kind of spiritual posture found among some who were the catalytic core—a spirit of urgency and audacity, an attitude of brokenness and desperation, a manner of prayer that could be daring and agonizing. These friends in the Hebrides called it travailing prayer, like the Holy Spirit groaning through them, they said, like a woman travailing in labor, like Paul in Galatians 4:19 travailing "as if in the pangs of childbirth that Christ might be formed in you."

The prayer of groaning, or travail, comes from a desperation not born of anxiety for a sought-after answer, but of determinedness to know God as the answer, come what may. Though the movement of God may be years in the future, history reveals the Holy Spirit's preference to grant the gravity of heaven to this manner of prayer.

God heard their groaning and he remembered his covenant with Abraham, with Isaac and with Jacob. So God looked on the Israelites and was concerned about them.

The Prayer

Lord Jesus, you are right here, right now. There are so many reasons why I fail to groan in prayer, but chief among them is the way I protect myself from the pain of others, even from my own pain. Awaken me to the deeper love of God, who runs with abandon into the face of darkness and whose suffering travail brings us saving grace. Right here, Jesus. Right now, Jesus. Amen.

The Questions

- Do you have any experience with the prayer of groaning or travail?
- Reflect on the difference between a desperation born of anxiety for answers and a desperation born of determinedness to know God as the answer.
- Why might it take a long season of groaning prayer before God seems to respond? How might we understand that?

31 The Prayer-Filled Life: On Fire but Not Consumed

EXODUS 3:4–10 | When the Lord saw that he had gone over to look, God called to him from within the bush, "Moses! Moses!"

And Moses said, "Here I am."

"Do not come any closer," God said. "Take off your sandals, for the place where you are standing is holy ground." Then he said, "I am the God of your father, the God of Abraham, the God of Isaac and the God of Jacob." At this, Moses hid his face, because he was afraid to look at God.

The Lord said, "I have indeed seen the misery of my people in Egypt. I have heard them crying out because of their slave drivers, and I am concerned about their suffering. So I have come down to rescue them from the hand of the Egyptians and to bring them up out of that land into a good and spacious land, a land flowing with milk and honey—the home of the Canaanites, Hittites, Amorites, Perizzites, Hivites and Jebusites. And now the cry of the Israelites has reached me, and I have seen the way the Egyptians are oppressing them. So now, go. I am sending you to Pharaoh to bring my people the Israelites out of Egypt."

Consider This

And Moses said, "Here I am."

Maybe you've heard the lines of the old hymn "When the Roll Is Called up Yonder." I think the bigger question asked by the Bible concerns who will respond when the roll is called down here.

Moses responded in good biblical form: "Here I am."

Today's text fascinates on so many levels. First, note the way God speaks.

"I am the God of your father . . . I have indeed seen . . . I have heard . . . I am concerned . . . I have come down to rescue them . . . to bring them up out of that land into a good and spacious land . . ."

So far, it sounds like we're about to get a show of divine proportions. God is about to take the stage and save the day. Then in a stunning turn of dialogue, God says this: *"So now, go. I am sending you to Pharaoh to bring my people the Israelites out of Egypt."*

All this about God's power and what God is going to do to rescue his people and bring down the most powerful nation on the planet and then this: *"So now, go. I am sending you to Pharaoh to bring my people the Israelites out of Egypt."*

God chooses an aging sheep herder as his ambassador to the most powerful man on earth. As my twelve-year-old son Sam, might say, "What the what?!"

Tomorrow we will get into the prayerful negotiation between Moses and God. Before ending, I want to reach back

a verse prior to where today's text begins: "Moses saw that though the bush was on fire it did not burn up. So Moses thought, 'I will go over and see this strange sight—why the bush does not burn up'" (Exod. 3:2–3).

A bush on fire in the desert was probably not that big of a deal. A bush on fire that is not burning up—that merits the double-take. On fire but not consumed. This is an image of what God would do with Moses' life. Moses by himself: an uninteresting scrub brush. Moses filled with the fullness of God: on fire but not consumed. Moses by himself: hardly worth noticing. Moses filled with the fullness of God: can't look away.

This is the vision of the prayer-filled life, which is the Spirit-filled life: on fire but not consumed.

Old Testament extraordinary is New Testament normal. Consider Pentecost, tongues of fire resting on Galilean fishermen—on fire but not consumed. Paul said it well: "But we have this treasure in jars of clay to show that this all-surpassing power is from God and not from us" (2 Cor. 4:7).

The Prayer

Lord Jesus, you are right here, right now. Your presence is the secret. I don't seek you for an answer. You are always the answer. Make of my life a luminous burning, a compelling vision of your presence, power, and possibility. Right here, Jesus. Right now, Jesus. Amen.

The Questions

- Put yourself in Moses' shoes. What was this experience like for him?
- What do you make of the statement, "Old Testament extraordinary is New Testament normal"?
- Are you compelled by the vision of becoming a person who is "on fire but not consumed"? What holds you back?

On Career-Ending Failures and New Beginnings

32

EXODUS 3:11–14; 4:1–3, 10–13 | But Moses said to God, "Who am I that I should go to Pharaoh and bring the Israelites out of Egypt?"

And God said, "I will be with you. And this will be the sign to you that it is I who have sent you: When you have brought the people out of Egypt, you will worship God on this mountain."

Moses said to God, "Suppose I go to the Israelites and say to them, 'The God of your fathers has sent me to you,' and they ask me, 'What is his name?' Then what shall I tell them?"

God said to Moses, "I AM WHO I AM. This is what you are to say to the Israelites: 'I AM has sent me to you.'" . . .

Moses answered, "What if they do not believe me or listen to me and say, 'The LORD did not appear to you'?"

Then the LORD said to him, "What is that in your hand?"

"A staff," he replied.

The LORD said, "Throw it on the ground." . . .

Moses said to the LORD, "Pardon your servant, Lord. I have never been eloquent, neither in the past nor since you have spoken to your servant. I am slow of speech and tongue."

The LORD said to him, "Who gave human beings their mouths? Who makes them deaf or mute? Who gives them sight or makes them blind? Is it not I, the LORD? Now go; I will help you speak and will teach you what to say."

But Moses said, "Pardon your servant, Lord. Please send someone else."

Consider This

I get a fair amount of reader e-mail. I got a note a couple of weeks back excoriating me for construing God's in-person conversation with Abraham as prayer. You remember the one, where Abraham seems to bargain with God over how many righteous people it would take to justify sparing Sodom from destruction. The reader thought this preposterous—that a face-to-face conversation between God and Abraham could be remotely related to prayer.

The underlying assumption seems to be that for prayer to be prayer, a person must be addressing a God who is somewhere other than, well, right here, right now.

We find ourselves in another extended negotiation; this time between God and Moses. Moses' moment, which surely he thought had passed, now presents itself again. Here we have an Israelite, miraculously spared from genocide as an infant, who grew up with all the privileges of a son in Pharaoh's palace. Imagine the promise and sense of destiny Moses once possessed. Then he killed the Egyptian slave master and, along with that, his future. For the next forty years, he wandered around behind a herd of sheep on the plains of Midian. "What a waste," his former friends and colleagues must have remarked to one another when talking about Moses.

I used to think it remarkable how Moses could so disqualify himself from God's clear calling and assignment for his life. As I look at it now, I see it differently. Of course Moses felt disqualified. I see him back then as a defeated man. At least his responses tell that story: *"Who am I . . . what shall I tell them . . . What if they do not believe me or listen . . . I am slow of speech and tongue . . . Please send someone else."*

Permit me a moment of pastoral intervention into what could be the lives of a considerable number of readers out there. No matter what failure (moral or otherwise), squelched calling, squandered opportunity, or missed moment may scream from your history, your future remains as bright as the promises of God. To borrow a phrase from the late, great Adoniram Judson: God is not done with you.

Moses, whose life was derailed by a moral failure of epic proportions—breaking the most egregious command he would later receive—became the most towering figure in the history of the world, second only to Jesus.

Maybe you walked off the playing field a long time ago. Might it be time to get back in the game? Your next and perhaps most important assignment of all could be a prayer away.

The Prayer

Lord Jesus, you are right here, right now. Thank you for never giving up on us. Thank you that you are bringing to completion the good work you have begun in me. Forgive me for disqualifying myself. Thank you that my worthiness comes from you and not from myself. Right here, Jesus. Right now, Jesus. Amen.

The Questions

- Do you see prayer as necessarily speaking to a God who is distant? Why not right here, right now?
- How do you see yourself in Moses?
- What do you feel disqualifies you from receiving a calling or assignment from Jesus? Are you ready to let that go?

On the Difference between Worrying Our Prayers and Praying Our Anxieties

33

EXODUS 5:22–23 | Moses returned to the LORD and said, "Why, Lord, why have you brought trouble on this people? Is this why you sent me? Ever since I went to Pharaoh to speak in your name, he has brought trouble on this people, and you have not rescued your people at all."

Consider This

Despite God's bold intervention and Moses' reluctant obedience, the plan does not seem to be working. Pharaoh is not getting on board. In the midst of it all, note these five key words:

Moses returned to the LORD.

This is prayer. I don't want to steal New Testament thunder, but Jesus told stories about a neighbor relentlessly knocking on a friend's door at midnight to get help for someone in need and about a widow who would not stop pestering an unjust judge for justice. He clearly associated prevailing faith with travailing prayer whose chief characteristic was "always praying and never giving up" (see Luke 18).

*"Why, Lord, why have you brought trouble on this people?
Is this why you sent me? Ever since I went to Pharaoh to speak
in your name, he has brought trouble on this people, and you
have not rescued your people at all."*

Remember, in the realm of prayer and faith, apparent
failure is par for the course. Success can't be tied to any particular outcome but to persistence itself. Remember, also, the
journey of maturing into a rich and wise faith is the process
of growing from seeking particular answers to prayers to
embracing Jesus as *the* answer.

Second, note the nature and tone of Moses' response
to God. Note the blaming here: *"Why, Lord, why have you
brought trouble on this people?"* And this feels like sarcasm:
"Is this why you sent me?"

*"Ever since I went to Pharaoh to speak in your name, he has
brought trouble on this people, and you have not rescued your
people at all."*

Translation: "Okay, I know Pharaoh is creating the problem
here, but you aren't doing anything about it." Let's not let the
effect of "at all" be lost on us either. It is as though Moses is
throwing his arms up in protest.

I point this out to say God can handle the full brunt of
our emotional volatility. In fact, I believe God welcomes
it. Disappointed with God? Don't hold back. In fact, to the
extent you do hold back, chances are your inner angst will
be visited either on some undeserving soul around you or on
yourself. I love the way the apostle Peter, who carried his fair
share of anxiety, instructs us, "Cast all your anxiety on him

because he cares for you" (1 Peter 5:7). There is a big difference between worrying our prayers and praying our anxieties. The former skirts the real honest truth. The latter trusts enough to keep it real.

The final observation I would make from today's text has to do with Moses' posture in this prayer. He still seems to be standing outside of the situation. Did you notice how he referred to the suffering Israelites?

"Why, Lord, why have you brought trouble on this people?"

He didn't claim them as "my people," did he?

"Ever since I went to Pharaoh to speak in your name, he has brought trouble on this people, and you have not rescued your people at all."

Note the "I" and "your" separation. Then he does it again, "this people." Finally he closes with "your people." It appears Moses, despite his reluctant involvement, still sees himself in a role somewhere between consultant and independent contractor. Far from an owner of "this people" and "this mission," he remains a bit of a hireling.

Let's be generous with Moses and with ourselves. In my judgment, Moses' audacity to bring the mess of his frustrated emotions before God prepares the way for his shift from disengaged messenger to sold-out martyr (which in the New Testament sense means not one who is willing to die for God but one who wills to die to himself). God is not looking for impressive witnesses who will tell people about God but for humble witnesses who will bear God's presence to others— be they powerful Pharaohs or poor beggars.

A wise person once said to me, "Conflict is the price of deepening intimacy." This holds true in our walk with God as well.

One of my favorite movies of all time is *The Apostle*, starring one of the great Arkansans, Robert Duval. He plays the part of Eulis "Sonny" Dewey, a Pentecostal preacher. There's a scene where he is up in the middle of the night pacing around his room praying aloud. To call it intense would be an understatement. At one point in the prayer he yells at God, "I'm confused! I'm mad! I love you, Lord. I love you, but I'm mad at you! I am mad at *you*!"

Sometimes, maybe more often than not, the most sanctified prayers are the most unfiltered, unsanctimonious prayers.

The Prayer

Lord Jesus, you are right here, right now. Thank you for inviting me to pray as I am and not as I should be. Give me the courage to be my unfiltered self in your presence. Open me up to my own raw emotions in the sanctuary of your presence. I am willing. Right here, Jesus. Right now, Jesus. Amen.

The Questions

- Have you ever expressed your anxiety in unfiltered and even what felt like risky ways before Jesus? What was that like? What is your level of access to your emotional life? How could bringing this before Jesus open you up?

- What do you make of this distinction between praying from the pain and struggle on the inside of a situation versus praying from the outside of it?
- Where are you in your Spirit-empowered sense of persistence and perseverance in prayer? Do you give up easily? Do you see the difference between willpower and the power of the Holy Spirit to help you?

Getting beyond Prayer as a Peewee Soccer Game

34

2 CHRONICLES 7:13–16 | "When I shut up the heavens so that there is no rain, or command locusts to devour the land or send a plague among my people, if my people, who are called by my name, will humble themselves and pray and seek my face and turn from their wicked ways, then I will hear from heaven, and I will forgive their sin and will heal their land. Now my eyes will be open and my ears attentive to the prayers offered in this place. I have chosen and consecrated this temple so that my Name may be there forever. My eyes and my heart will always be there."

Consider This

As we began this series on prayer, it was tempting to do a Google search on "prayers in the Old Testament" and go from one to the next to the next with these daily entries. After all, there are hundreds of prayers in the Old Testament. It would have been a very tactical approach, and people love tactical approaches.

So why didn't I take that direction? Thanks for asking. It's because I am convinced our greatest challenge is not at the level of tactics. When it comes to prayer, conventional wisdom says if we can just get more people praying more prayers for more time we will win. I've seen enough of this to know that we can get more people praying more prayers for more time and the outcome turns out to be just more people praying more prayers for more time.

Friends, the problem is not at the level of tactical engagement (though we do have problems there). The greater challenge, as it relates to our personal and collective life of prayer, comes at the level of vision, mission, and strategy. If we do not comprehend the vision, which is a visual articulation of the preferred future, we will not understand our mission, which is the clearly stated purpose for our existence. If we do not understand our mission, there is no way to think strategically about how to implement it. And in the absence of strategy, we move from tactic to tactic to tactic, fighting over the color of the carpet in the sanctuary and who should have keys to the fellowship hall.

Admittedly, words like *vision, mission, strategy*, and *tactics* are twentieth-century business terms; however, they have ancient precursors. It's why we spent so much time in Genesis 1 and 2 in this prayer series.

We needed to see the vision, which in biblical terms meant we needed to first hear the vision from God's very Word. If our prayers are not anchored in the very essence of Eden, they will, at best, attach themselves to some alternative (and usually seductive) vision of prosperity or, at worst, devolve into corporate liturgical mumblings.

If we do not understand our mission of walking with the Father in the power of the Spirit as the regents and viceroys of Jesus, stewarding his grace for all of creation, our prayers will largely serve an agenda of self-protection and the advance of our own agendas and ambitions.

Without the mission of God, we are destined to substitute all manner of strategic initiatives to accomplish our own individual and tribal missions to find life, liberty, and the pursuit of happiness, whatever we interpret those words to mean. Our strategies will be built on the premise of scarcity rather than abundance, and our political ideologies will guide us far more than our theological convictions; often with the former masquerading as the latter.

To pray in the way of Jesus assumes we already see the vision, get the mission, and understand the strategies. Imagine being dropped onto the playing field of a World Cup Soccer game and being told to "just play." And did I mention that you don't really understand soccer? This is the equivalent of focusing on prayer at the tactical level. Sure, you can run around the field, wear yourself out, maybe even kick the ball, and feel like you've done something. But really?

We have mistakenly assumed that because we can read and God is powerful that we just kind of get it. The result is in our efforts to pray, much of the church looks like a peewee soccer game. You been to one of those lately? It amounts to about eighteen kids blobbed together futilely following a ball around a field and mostly kicking each other. While that cute spectacle must touch God's heart to see, surely he grows impatient after a hundred years. It's time to grow up, church. It's no one's fault. It's just time.

Tomorrow we will reconvene somewhere near the modern-day city of Cairo, Egypt, where we will explore prayer and divine deliverance from a vision, mission, strategy, and tactical dimension. I am no expert, so prepare to tolerate my peewee-level efforts. I promise I will try not to kick you.

The Prayer

Lord Jesus, you are right here, right now. You are our great teacher when it comes to prayer and everything else. Thank you for tolerating my slowness to take this seriously. And thank you that taking it seriously really isn't even the point. Thank you that you want me to wake up and show up and pray with you, as long as it takes. Right here, Jesus. Right now, Jesus. Amen.

The Questions

- Do you find the vision, mission, strategy, and tactics framework at all helpful or instructive when it comes to understanding prayer? How?

- Where do you need the most help? The big vision informing prayer? Mission? Strategy? Tactics?
- How do you relate to this peewee soccer game image as relates to the kingdom calling to enter into a life of prayer? How does it motivate you?

Why Prayer Cannot Be Reverse Delegation

35

EXODUS 3:7–8; 16–17 | The Lord said, "I have indeed seen the misery of my people in Egypt. I have heard them crying out because of their slave drivers, and I am concerned about their suffering. So I have come down to rescue them from the hand of the Egyptians and to bring them up out of that land into a good and spacious land, a land flowing with milk and honey—the home of the Canaanites, Hittites, Amorites, Perizzites, Hivites and Jebusites. . . .

"Go, assemble the elders of Israel and say to them, 'The Lord, the God of your fathers—the God of Abraham, Isaac and Jacob—appeared to me and said: I have watched over you and have seen what has been done to you in Egypt. And I have promised to bring you up out of your misery in Egypt into the land of the Canaanites, Hittites, Amorites, Perizzites, Hivites and Jebusites—a land flowing with milk and honey.'"

Consider This

The Israelites faced in ancient Egypt what we would today call a full-blown humanitarian crisis. God heard their cries. He chose Moses as his spokesperson. Notice, however, what God does not do in the face of a humanitarian crisis. God does not provide humanitarian aid. Instead, he provides divine deliverance.

It may sound wrong to say this, and to be sure it feels challenging to write it, but the answer to a humanitarian crisis is not humanitarian aid to alleviate suffering. The answer is divine deliverance from suffering into flourishing. Okay, before anyone picks up something to throw at me, hear me out. Am I saying humanitarian aid is out of order? Absolutely not. It is a thoroughgoing good, essential, biblical, Christian human response. Humanitarian aid, however, is not a solution to a problem brought on by sin, darkness, death, and evil. It is a mercy but not a solution.

Notice the way God reasserts his vision for human flourishing.

"So I have come down to rescue them from the hand of the Egyptians and to bring them up out of that land into a good and spacious land, a land flowing with milk and honey . . .

"And I have promised to bring you up out of your misery in Egypt into the land . . . a land flowing with milk and honey."

The vision is Eden, but not a nostalgic pining for the good old days and the way things used to be. This is about the new Eden, also known as the new creation. The will of God is not to make human suffering more tolerable. It is to deliver all of creation from evil into the kingdom of God, on earth as it is in heaven.

Somewhere along the way over the last few complicated centuries the focus of the Christian faith shifted from "on earth as it is in heaven" to "leaving earth in order to get to heaven." It behooves us to ask, What on earth is heaven? Heaven is the unabated, unadulterated, presence of God in the place where human flourishing displaces human suffering. This is why God created the earth as . . . a land flowing with milk and honey.

So what does any of this have to do with prayer? As long as we think of prayer as a tactical practice or, worse, a religious exercise, prayer will continue to be the thing we turn to when nothing else works. It will be our way of literally throwing our hands up and delegating the problem to God.

The answer is not more and more expressions of prayer or more singing. Neither is the answer more humanitarian aid. The answer is divine deliverance via human agency. God willed to deliver the Israelites out of bondage and into flourishing, and he determined to do it through Moses. God did not choose Moses because Moses was praying. He came to Moses because Israel was praying, and he came to Moses because Moses was uniquely situated and divinely prepared to walk with God, as a coregent and viceroy, and participate in the Spirit's power to deliver God's people from evil and suffering.

Clearly Moses wanted to delegate the problem. He would have been happy to lead a prayer campaign back at the ranch.

I am the same way. I see prayer primarily as reverse delegation, a way of asking God to solve problems I either can't solve or in which I don't want to get overly involved. I say I'll pray for you when I can't really help you.

I'm coming to believe God's response to this vision of prayer is, "Don't bother. If you don't want to get involved at the ground level of the divine deliverance movement called my church, stop fooling yourself. Just get back to your Netflix."

Prayer must take on a far more comprehensive structure in our lives and communities. Prayer, as vision, opens a way of participation in the supernatural vision of God for human flourishing. Prayer, as mission, unites us into a place of unified agreement, together with God, around his mission in the world. Prayer, as strategy, coalesces all manner of grace gifts and spiritual discernment to bind evil, spy out the giants in the land, move mountains, and reclaim territory. And prayer, as tactical engagement, becomes a way of walking around in the work-a-day world as bearers of the presence of Jesus, doing both mighty and mundane things in his name, every single day.

I have always been drawn to this mystical yet practical thought about prayer by the late Thomas Merton. Let's give him the last word today:

> If our prayer is the expression of a deep and grace-inspired desire for newness of life—and not the mere blind attachment to what has always been familiar and "safe"—God will act in us and through us to renew the

church by preparing, in prayer, what we cannot yet imagine or understand.[6]

The Prayer

Lord Jesus, you are right here, right now. Open my heart, mind, spirit, and my physical body to be stretched beyond my very limited understanding of what I think prayer is. I can be so attached to what is predictable and safe. I'm tired of that. I am ready for a new and living way. That way is you. I just know it. Right here, Jesus. Right now, Jesus. Amen.

The Questions

- Are you willing to tolerate the frustration brought on by this series on prayer or are you ready to quit? Be honest.
- Where might you have a "blind attachment to what has always been familiar and 'safe'" as it relates to prayer? Are you willing to be broken out of that way? Be honest.
- Are you willing to dig in at a deeper level into what the Holy Spirit may want to teach you in the coming days? It's okay, if not; it may not be the time right now. Just be honest.

---

6   Thomas Merton, *Contemplation in a World of Action*, 2nd ed. (University of Notre Dame, 1998), n. p.

36 The Most Simple and Complex Prayer of All

EXODUS 5:2 | Pharaoh said, "Who is the LORD, that I should obey him and let Israel go? I do not know the LORD and I will not let Israel go."

Consider This

I want to take stock of the complexity of divine deliverance by looking at this Exodus scenario. For starters, we are no longer talking about the extended family of Abraham caught in a tight spot and needing help. In Exodus, we face the mass enslavement of an entire nation of people. We have hundreds of thousands of men, women, and children bound in a tyrannical, unjust, cruel, and inhumane system.

Did I mention this had gone on for decades, if not centuries? Not only did a people need to be delivered, but persons needed deliverance. Ultimately, while the former would prove successful, the latter would not. It would take forty years in the wilderness to finally bury all the former slaves who could never leave slavery and to form new generations who could begin to receive the promises of God. Deliverance is a multi-generational project. It is as true now as it was then, and we are all somewhere in that process within our own generations (see also Exodus 20:4–6).

Meanwhile, back at the ranch, Moses and Aaron first delivered the good news to the Israelite elders. They told them everything God said. They even performed the signs in front of them. In Exodus 4:31 we are told, "and they believed. And when they heard that the LORD was concerned about them and had seen their misery, they bowed down and worshiped." All good, right? Not on your life. *Piece of cake*, they must have thought. Not so fast. Next stop Pharaoh's palace.

"Afterward Moses and Aaron went to Pharaoh and said, 'This is what the LORD, the God of Israel, says: "Let my people go, so that they may hold a festival to me in the wilderness."'" (Exod. 5:1).

Pharaoh said, "Who is the LORD, that I should obey him and let Israel go? I do not know the LORD and I will not let Israel go."

Not only did he categorically reject the request, he did this: "Pharaoh said, 'Lazy, that's what you are—lazy! That is why you keep saying, "Let us go and sacrifice to the LORD." Now get to work. You will not be given any straw, yet you must produce your full quota of bricks'" (Exod. 5:17–18).

On top of making their treatment more inhumane, Pharaoh publicly shamed the Israelites, adding insult to injury. From Eden to Egypt, shame always leads to blame. In response to this, the Israelite overseers ran back to Moses and Aaron with this stinging word: "May the LORD look on you and judge you! You have made us obnoxious to Pharaoh and his officials and have put a sword in their hand to kill us" (5:21).

Moses then visited his angst and frustration on God, in response to which God reiterated the resolve of his promise of deliverance. Moses went back to the Israelites to share the good news of God's promised deliverance only to find this:

"Moses reported this to the Israelites, but they did not listen to him because of their discouragement and harsh labor" (Exod. 6:9).

So far, we have Pharaoh, Pharaoh's minions, the Israelite slaves, their overseers, Moses, Aaron, and God. We have suffering, oppression, shame, anxiety, discouragement, depression, and despair. When the threat of deliverance is whispered into this kind of setting, look for things to blow up and get a lot worse—the Word of God notwithstanding. Just as ground seems to be gained, the oppression grows stronger.

Deliverance is complex. Why? Because the status quo always has the "mo" (as in momentum). As my friend, Maxie Dunnam, says, "Most people prefer the hell of a predictable situation rather than the joy of an unpredictable one." People in prison often return to prison. People in addiction often refuse help. God respects human freedom and has chosen to work within the myriad complexities it presents in so many situations. Divine deliverance is the strategic intervention of the Holy Spirit working through human agents for the sake of the freedom and flourishing of people who are oppressed and bound. It happens through prayerful discernment and bold obedience.

As we are seeing in Egypt, so we see today, things often have to get a lot worse before they begin to get better. As we will see, it is messy and fraught with conflict and controversy. In addition to being a divinely canonized historical story of the mighty acts of God, the Exodus provides tremendous wisdom for the present-day work of prayer and deliverance.

Who knew? The well-known petition from the Lord's Prayer, "deliver us from the evil one" might all at once be the most simple and the most complex prayer of all (Matt. 6:13).

The Prayer

Lord Jesus, you are right here, right now. You are our great deliverer, one greater than Moses, who with a mighty hand and an outstretched arm, in the grip of the cross, delivered us from darkness to light and from death to life. Fill me with confidence in your power to deliver completely those who trust in you. Right here, Jesus. Right now, Jesus. Amen.

The Questions

- Have you ever been in a situation that called for divine deliverance? What stands out in your remembrance about the complexities of that situation?
- Are there strongholds in your life from which you need deliverance? Have you ever shared those with anyone else?
- What "hell of a predictable situation" do you find yourself or someone you love stuck in? How are you learning to pray more strategically for yourself or them?

37

The Prayer of Deliverance: From the Bondage of Slavery to the Bonding of Worship

EXODUS 3:12 | And God said, "I will be with you. And this will be the sign to you that it is I who have sent you: When you have brought the people out of Egypt, you will worship God on this mountain."

Consider This

The sign of deliverance is worship.

True deliverance is not the change from this condition to that condition but the movement from slavery to freedom and it is signaled by the unfettered worship of the delivered. There are many who have reined in an addiction to some substance but remain enslaved. Though they have moved from uncontrolled substance abuse to abstinence, so many have not yet experienced deliverance from slavery to freedom. They may seem to have gotten out of Egypt, but Egypt is not yet out of them.

The sign of deliverance is the worship of the only true and living God who, I might add, is Jesus Christ. Every other god is a false god which demands total allegiance and delivers slavish attachment. I find it interesting how the conversation around addiction centers around the language of recovery rather than deliverance. Don't get me wrong, I have enormous appreciation for the addiction-recovery movement. My problem is their starting place. They do not begin with the vision of divine freedom, but rather with unmanageable addiction. As a result, they do not end with divine freedom, but managed addiction. (Just so you know that I know, I recognize it's a lot more complex than that and my rhetoric may be overstated and unfair, so don't let that cause you to miss the thrust of today's reflection.)

Now, may I be bold with you? The human condition is slavery, whether voluntary or involuntary. Human beings, by nature, will have a master, even if we believe that master to be ourselves. God, by nature, will only be the master of those who willingly surrender their allegiance to him, but the beauty of this surrender is the way he returns his allegiance to his followers. Deliverance is rescue from the bondage of a false god and the restoration of bonding with the true God.

No less than ten times we see some form of this petition from Moses to Pharaoh.

"Then the Lord said to Moses, 'Go to Pharaoh and say to him, "This is what the Lord says: Let my people go, so that they may worship me"'" (Exod. 8:1).

Note the twofold movement: 1. Let my people go. 2. So that they may worship me. 1. Release from bondage. 2. Return to bonding (i.e., worship).

What if we practiced this very form of prayer as deliverance? So often we say our prayers to God, which is fine, but I wonder what impact it might have if we began speaking our prayers in the form of the Word of God directly into the face of evil.

"'This is what the LORD says: Let my people go, so that they may worship me.'"

How about like this? "This is what the Lord says to you [name the oppressor or bondage or slave holder here], let [name the one being oppressed or enslaved here] go so that they may worship me."

Don't be surprised when it doesn't happen the first or second or hundredth time. And don't be shocked when all hell breaks loose in response to the rebellion of darkness. Take comfort from Moses, who never gave in until Pharaoh gave up.

Every time we gather in the fellowship of the New Room—a conference hosted by Seedbed—we end our time with a raucous singing of what we call our fight song. It's one of the great hymns of deliverance in the history of the church. Written by Charles Wesley, this great anthem of the gospel, "And Can It Be," never disappoints.

Something about a song of deliverance takes us inside of itself and hides us in the shelter of the Most High God. Songs of deliverance are poetry carried by the Spirit of God into the realm of prophecy. We do not so much sing these songs as they sing us. By the time the fourth verse comes around, the atmosphere in the room is near the breaking point as we sing:

> Long my imprisoned spirit lay
> Fast-bound in sin and nature's night;
> Thine eye diffused a quick'ning ray,

I woke the dungeon flamed with light;
My chains fell off, my heart was free;
I rose, went forth and followed Thee.

That last line is not even sung. It's bellowed. Every hand in the room lifts like a rocket en route to the heavens. And the sound of chains hitting the floor is palpable.

My chains fell off, my heart was free; I rose, went forth and followed Thee.

From the millennial who doesn't care much for hymns to my mother who had never heard the song before to the Salvation Army bass-drumming grandmother who has sung it all her life—all of them will tell you it was worth the whole trip just to sing that song.

"'This is what the LORD says: Let my people go, so that they may worship me.'"

And if you haven't signed up for this year's New Room Conference, I don't know what else to say but, "There's still time." If you like the Daily Text, these are your people. This is your conference.

Come on!

The Prayer

Lord Jesus, you are right here, right now. You fill me with songs of deliverance. In fact, you are my song of deliverance. Help me hear that song deeper and deeper. Teach me to sing it into the face of darkness and evil. You are my deliverer. Right here, Jesus. Right now, Jesus. Amen.

The Questions

- Did you cross the line today and commit to joining us for the New Room Conference this fall?
- How do you see the difference between praying to God to deliver a person and speaking the word of God's deliverance to an oppressor as a form of prayer?
- What do you make of this transformation from bondage to bonding? How are they related? How are they different in your experience?

38 | When It's Time to Stop Crying Out and Start Moving On

EXODUS 14:10–16 | As Pharaoh approached, the Israelites looked up, and there were the Egyptians, marching after them. They were terrified and cried out to the LORD. They said to Moses, "Was it because there were no graves in Egypt that you brought us to the desert to die? What have you done to us by bringing us out of Egypt? Didn't we say to you in Egypt, 'Leave us alone; let us serve the Egyptians'? It would have been better for us to serve the Egyptians than to die in the desert!"

Moses answered the people, "Do not be afraid. Stand firm and you will see the deliverance the LORD will bring you today. The Egyptians you see today you will never see again. The LORD will fight for you; you need only to be still."

Then the Lᴏʀᴅ said to Moses, "Why are you crying out to me? Tell the Israelites to move on. Raise your staff and stretch out your hand over the sea to divide the water so that the Israelites can go through the sea on dry ground."

Consider This

Today's text shows us the messy truth about deliverance in the real world. Finally, the Israelites were outside the city limits. They carried with them the ancient equivalent of Fort Knox in Egyptian wealth. In the end, after all the pleadings and all the plagues, the Egyptians paid them to leave. As Pharaoh was want to do, though, he changed his mind. Look how quickly the patient changed their tune.

They said to Moses, "Was it because there were no graves in Egypt that you brought us to the desert to die? What have you done to us by bringing us out of Egypt? Didn't we say to you in Egypt, 'Leave us alone; let us serve the Egyptians'? It would have been better for us to serve the Egyptians than to die in the desert!"

Moses puts on his Braveheart and dials up his best William Wallace. *"Do not be afraid. Stand firm and you will see the deliverance the Lᴏʀᴅ will bring you today. The Egyptians you see today you will never see again. The Lᴏʀᴅ will fight for you; you need only to be still."*

That must have gone over like a lead balloon. Then the Lord intervenes with this word to Moses: *"Why are you crying out to me? Tell the Israelites to move on."*

I have a feeling this is how the Lord feels most of the time when it comes to his people (a.k.a. us). *"Why are you crying out to me?"*

It's one of my favorite analogies and I overuse it, but it is as if we keep asking God to write the check. All the while God is saying, "Cash it!" The check was written at Easter. Further, at Pentecost, he put more wealth in our proverbial bank than we could spend in ten thousand lifetimes. We are loaded and all the while we parade around like paupers. Divine deliverance is at our fingertips, yet we believe God wants to see a demonstration of desperation from us.

"Why are you crying out to me?" The operative word comes in the next sentence.

"Move on."

You know we talk a lot in our work about awakening and sowing for a great awakening. I am increasingly of a mind that this word from today's text is for us.

"Why are you crying out to me? Tell [my people] to move on."

In this country, and in many others around the world, we live in a time where we face an impassable Red Sea on one side and the raging chariots of Pharaoh's army on the other. Many of us find ourselves grumbling over all that has been lost and wanting to return to a bygone era. Many others are still betting the farm on presidential politics and Supreme Court justice. Many more are neck-deep in denominational reorganization and ecclesial hand-wringing. In the midst of this, many call us to our knees, rightly pointing us to God, urging us to be still and wait for the Lord; cautioning that human effort might supplant supernatural deliverance. Meanwhile, I wonder if the word for our time just might be, *"Why are you crying out to me? Tell [my people] to move on."*

After all, Jesus Christ *is* risen from the dead. The Holy Spirit *is* being poured out on the whole creation. Sin has lost its power. Death has lost its sting (see 1 Corinthians 15:55–57). He who is in us is greater than he who is in the world. We have the extraordinarily incredible gifts of the Word, the Spirit, the church, and the kingdom, literally, at hand.

What if a great awakening and all the divine deliverance it would entail waits on us to wake up to this word: *"Why are you crying out to me? Tell [my people] to move on."*?

The Prayer

Lord Jesus, you are right here, right now. You have done so much—everything, really. The first great awakening was your resurrection from the dead. The second great awakening was the sending of your Spirit. Forgive me for somehow expecting you to do those things again—to give what you have already given and keep giving. Awaken me to the full reality of it all. Right here, Jesus. Right now, Jesus. Amen.

The Questions

- What do you make of this analogy of asking God to write the check while God asks us to "cash it"?
- Creation. Exodus. Resurrection. Pentecost. Are we crying out for God to do something else? Are we waiting on God? Or is God waiting on us?

- What would it look like in our Red Sea moment to stop crying out and start moving on?

39 | Why We Don't Know Much about History

EXODUS 15:1–2 | Then Moses and the Israelites sang this song to the LORD: "I will sing to the LORD, for he is highly exalted. Both horse and driver he has hurled into the sea.

"The LORD is my strength and my defense; he has become my salvation. He is my God, and I will praise him, my father's God, and I will exalt him."

Consider This

We come to our last week of the series on prayer and the Old Testament. Our next few weeks will continue the series on prayer but this time in the New Testament. I know, we have hardly covered the Old Testament. As I noted earlier, rather than taking a more technical approach and jumping from prayer to prayer, I wanted us to take a deeper dive into the deeper fundamentals of prayer as we learn from creation (Genesis) and redemption (Exodus). Rather than thin principles about prayer, I wanted us to delve into thick paradigms for prayer. Still we have hardly scratched the surface.

It brings to mind questions I recently received from a Daily Text reader: Why is the book of Exodus important for me today? What does it have to do with my life?

Let me bring it down to one word: *memory*. We who live in the early twenty-first century have an anemic understanding of history. It's not so much that we don't know our history as we don't grasp the concept of history. History, and particularly biblical history, is not a subject to be studied. It is a memory to be inhabited. Abraham and Sarah are not ancient biblical characters (okay, they are). They are our parents. To say that this is our story is not to say this is our history, which has a way of distancing it from us. To claim it as our story is to do just the opposite from distancing. It is to bring it close, to make it our memory.

Fast-forward with me some forty years later to the book of Deuteronomy. The people of Israel were finally preparing to enter the promised land. Moses addressed them with these words: "The LORD our God made a covenant with us at Horeb. It was not with our ancestors that the LORD made this covenant, but with us, with all of us who are alive here today" (5:2–3).

Actually, no. The people Moses was talking to were not present at Horeb (or they were only knee-high to a grasshopper). In Deuteronomy, Moses brought the history near in such a way as to brand it in the memory of a people who could not technically remember it. This is why the Passover is so critical for Israel. Passover, like the Lord's Supper, brings the history near—not just by retelling it but by eating and drinking and singing and embracing.

So what does memory have to do with prayer? Everything. Our living memory determines the imaginative capacity with which we can pray. For better or worse, our imagination does not come out of thin air. It comes directly from our memory. If we do not remember the words and deeds of the One in whose image we are made, we simply can't imagine how those words and deeds have any bearing or relevance in our lives today.

It's another reason we sing this story. The Israelites hadn't even caught their breath from the Red Sea deliverance and they were already singing.

"I will sing to the Lord, for he is highly exalted. Both horse and driver he has hurled into the sea."

Look through the rest of the Bible and notice how many times this ancient history was brought into present-day memory. Every time it did, it exploded in the imagination of the singing and praying people.

Don't believe me? Consider one of the most popular worship songs of the last several years. It's a song people don't just sing. They inhabit it. The song is called "No Longer Slaves" and both theologically and melodically must be one of the most compelling songs of deliverance written in the last hundred years. There comes a place late in the song, just when we think it is over, when we find ourselves transported to the shoreline of the Red Sea:

"You split the sea so I could walk right through it. My fears were drowned in perfect love. You rescued me and I will stand and sing, 'I am a child of God.'"[7]

That's how it works. When deep in our soul biblical memory touches holy imagination, prayer takes on a new essence. Our broken history becomes a redeemed future. We begin to know in a new way who we really are and why we are here.

At this place, our prayers become our songs and together they narrate the story of deliverance into new generations.

"In your unfailing love you will lead the people you have redeemed. In your strength you will guide them to your holy dwelling" (Exod. 15:13).

The Prayer

Lord Jesus, you are right here, right now. Yours is the story which has become our song. Bring your Word and Spirit into my life as my memory and my imagination. Right here, Jesus. Right now, Jesus. Amen.

The Questions

- What challenges you about this idea of making the biblical story your memory?
- So why is the story of Genesis and Exodus, creation and redemption, important for your life today?

---

7   "No Longer Slaves" written by Jonathan David Helser, Brian Johnson, and Joel Case © 2014 Bethel Music Publishing (ASCAP). All rights reserved. Used by permission.

• How is your praying imagination stirred and stoked by the story of Passover and the Red Sea? How might it become so?

40 Prayer as Problem Solving or Presence Seeking

EXODUS 15:22–24 | Then Moses led Israel from the Red Sea and they went into the Desert of Shur. For three days they traveled in the desert without finding water. When they came to Marah, they could not drink its water because it was bitter. (That is why the place is called Marah.) So the people grumbled against Moses, saying, "What are we to drink?"

Consider This

Why does everything have to be so hard? Surely the Israelites must have wondered. They had just come through a period of harsh oppression on steroids, been delivered from the plague of death and the Red Sea, and all of this only to die of dehydration in the desert. Three days is the upper limit without water. Imagine the relief they felt when they came to the waters at Marah and then the devastation at not being able to drink it.

A lot of people reading this (present company included) have the same question: Why does everything have to be so hard? Doesn't divine deliverance make things easier? Divine deliverance makes things better, eventually, but easier may not be in the cards. Slavery, after all, has its advantages. Most prisons guarantee three square meals a day. While we weren't made for slavery or prison, neither were we made for ease and comfort. Here's the hard thing. What if much of the ease and comfort we in America are accustomed to is another form of slavery?

I think there is a lot in me that still expects life to be easy, and so my continual quest looks like striving to get to that place. In my early twenties, a friend gave me the book *The Road Less Traveled* by M. Scott Peck. The book represents his quest as a psychiatrist to make sense of life. Though the book holds a lot of wisdom, it is an amalgamation of psychology, Zen Buddhism, self-help theories, and a sprinkling of Christian theology. I am primarily indebted to the book for its opening paragraph, which says:

> Life is difficult. This is a great truth, one of the greatest truths. It is a great truth because once we truly see this truth, we transcend it. Once we truly know that life is difficult—once we truly understand and accept it—then life is no longer difficult. Because once it is accepted, the fact that life is difficult no longer matters.[8]

Jesus said as much, didn't he? "I have told you these things, so that in me you may have peace. In this world you will have trouble. But take heart! I have overcome the world" (John 16:33).

---

8   M. Scott Peck, *The Road Less Traveled, 25th Anniversary Edition: A New Psychology of Love, Traditional Values, and Spiritual Growth* (New York: Simon and Schuster, 2002), 15.

We spend enormous amounts of energy to try and make life less difficult. In fact, I suspect much of our agenda in prayer is aimed at the end of solving problems. The evidence of this is how much time we spend grumbling about our problems at someone else, be it the president or the Democrats or the bishops or those idiots at headquarters.

What if our problems are not meant to drive us toward solutions but into the presence of God? Think about it. To what end are we driving—a problem-free life of ease without difficulty? Okay, yes! Do we really believe that is an option? Or is the endgame a life of knowing God as Deliverer and Provider and Healer and Lover of our souls and learning to trust these realities even when they don't seem present or on our timetable or according to our design?

The journey of growing up as a human being leads to the place where we cease to be consumed with seeking relief from our problems and instead learn to pursue the refuge of God's presence where we discover that he is himself our relief. One of the outcomes of this is we become the sort of people whose presence becomes a kind of prayerful refuge of relief for others in their problems. Instead of retreating from them with promises to pray for them, we run toward them with outstretched arms of mercy, grace, and love—knowing that God will show them his enough-ness through the enormity of our limitations.

Don't hear me wrong. God loves it when we pray for each other. He rises up and calls us blessed when we become bearers of his presence to each other.

Meanwhile, here's the scene back at Marah: *So the people grumbled against Moses, saying, "What are we to drink?"*

It's interesting to me how the Israelites cried out to God in their slavery, but now in their freedom they would grumble against Moses. I really don't think they much expected to be delivered from slavery and into God's presence. I suspect they just wanted their slavery to be easier. Deliverance comes with responsibility. Relief from problems, well . . . is just a break until the next problems show up. "Then Moses cried out to the Lord, and the Lord showed him a piece of wood. He threw it into the water, and the water became fit to drink" (Exod. 15:25).

The Lord wants to solve our problems. Remember, he wants our flourishing. His will is for a much deeper flourishing, one not dependent on our circumstances but on his nearness. Check this out:

> There the Lord issued a ruling and instruction for them and put them to the test: He said, "If you listen carefully to the Lord your God and do what is right in his eyes, if you pay attention to his commands and keep all his decrees, I will not bring on you any of the diseases I brought on the Egyptians, for I am the Lord, who heals you." (Exod. 15:26)

The test is growing in a bonded trust in his I Am-ness as our very health and wellness rather than our testing God as a health benefits provider. Will our praying agenda be geared around problem solving or presence seeking?

Today the problem is drinking water. Tomorrow we camp in a veritable oasis.

"Then they came to Elim, where there were twelve springs and seventy palm trees, and they camped there near the water" (Exod. 15:27).

Next week the problem is food. The week after . . .

When will we learn, he is all we need?

The Prayer

Lord Jesus, you are right here, right now. When will I finally learn that you don't have the answers to my problems but you are the answer? In your presence is more than everything I want and need. In the face of all our challenges, you are the One who has overcome the world. Above all, train my heart to seek you simply for who you are. Right here, Jesus. Right now, Jesus. Amen.

The Questions

- What if much of the ease and comfort we in America are accustomed to is another form of slavery?
- What if our problems are not meant to drive us toward solutions but into the presence of God?
- Do you want your problems to be easier or do you really want deliverance and all that entails?

The Unconventional Warfare of Prayer

41

EXODUS 17:8–9 | The Amalekites came and attacked the Israelites at Rephidim. Moses said to Joshua, "Choose some of our men and go out to fight the Amalekites. Tomorrow I will stand on top of the hill with the staff of God in my hands."

Consider This

In today's text we see a picture of what intercession looks like. In the blue corner we have the attacking Amalekites. In the red corner we have Joshua and the Israelites. On top of the hill we have General Moses and two lieutenant colonels in Aaron and Hur.

Traditional military strategy would tend to put all the emphasis on Joshua and his army. This battle seems to rise and fall on other factors; namely, the position of Moses' staff. When his staff is raised up, Israel prevails. When the staff is lowered, Israel loses ground. The staff is not magic, rather it is a symbol of the power of God.

> As long as Moses held up his hands, the Israelites were winning, but whenever he lowered his hands, the Amalekites were winning. When Moses' hands grew tired, they took a stone and put it under him and he sat on it. Aaron and Hur held his hands up—one on one

side, one on the other—so that his hands remained
steady till sunset. (Exod. 17:11–12)

Why didn't God sovereignly cause Israel to win the battle?
I think it's because God wills to work with, in, and through
people. Intercessors, servants who stand between God and
people, play key roles in the kingdom of God. It's interesting
how Moses is not on the battlefield, yet he plays the deter-
minative role in the battle. Moses does nothing of apparent
significance or perceived strategic importance. He raises
a piece of wood in the air. Moses participates in the most
essential secret strategy of identifying himself completely
with God. He stands in a place where he can take no credit
for the outcome, yet without his standing there the outcome
would go the other way.

In this way, intercessors occupy the most secret and most
strategic place of all in the economy of God's kingdom. Their
job description, if you will, is to identify so completely with
the interest of the Holy Spirit in any given assignment they
receive they can tend to lose touch with their own interest. As
a result, intercessors can tend to be some of the most misunderstood people in the kingdom. And yes, they can be more
than a little bit weird at times.

While intercessory prayer is a general and broad practice
in the church, the role of intercessor is unique and quite
specific. It is both a gifting and calling. You tend to know it if
you have it. It can't be taught, but it can be trained.

They exemplify and embody two texts from the New
Testament in extraordinary ways:

"But when you pray, go into your room, close the door and pray to your Father, who is unseen. Then your Father, who sees what is done in secret, will reward you." (Matt. 6:6)

"But we have this treasure in jars of clay to show that this all-surpassing power is from God and not from us." (2 Cor. 4:7)

There is another role identified in the text that seems equally critical to the role of the intercessor. Let's call it the intercessors for the intercessor. Aaron and Hur came alongside Moses and supported him in his intercessory role. In fact, had they not held up his arms, Israel would have lost the battle.

All of this reveals to us the nature of the body of Christ. No one's role or assignment is more important than anyone else's, yet each is uniquely significant and strategic. No Joshua = no victory. No army = no victory. No Moses = no victory. No Aaron and Hur = no victory. Victory came from God through all of them working together in a powerfully unified fashion. In the body of Christ there is no support staff. Everyone is a servant.

One more word about Aaron and Hur. Everyone needs an Aaron and Hur in his/her life and everyone needs to be an Aaron and Hur in someone else's life. Galatians 6:2 says, "Bear one another's burdens, and so fulfill the law of Christ" (ESV).

Finally, note the way Moses celebrated the victory. I'm sure he expressed gratitude to Aaron and Hur and high-fived

Joshua and his warriors. It would have been tempting for Moses to take a little credit and share in the glory, especially after being so vociferously criticized earlier. He resisted that temptation.

"Moses built an altar and called it The LORD is my Banner" (Exod. 17:15).

The Prayer

Lord Jesus, you are right here, right now. You are my banner. Teach me the meaning of this truth and grace me with the humility to live and move and have my being underneath this banner. Right here, Jesus. Right now, Jesus. Amen.

The Questions

- Do you have a sense that you are an intercessor or have this unique kind of gifting and calling in prayer? What has that been like for you?
- Do you have an Aaron and Hur in your life? Are you serving in an ongoing way as an Aaron or Hur in someone else's life? How is that going?
- What do you make of the way there was no hero in this battle because everyone played a uniquely strategic role?

Prayer as a Campout in the Sanctuary of God's Presence

42

EXODUS 33:7–11 | Now Moses used to take a tent and pitch it outside the camp some distance away, calling it the "tent of meeting." Anyone inquiring of the Lord would go to the tent of meeting outside the camp. And whenever Moses went out to the tent, all the people rose and stood at the entrances to their tents, watching Moses until he entered the tent. As Moses went into the tent, the pillar of cloud would come down and stay at the entrance, while the Lord spoke with Moses. Whenever the people saw the pillar of cloud standing at the entrance to the tent, they all stood and worshiped, each at the entrance to their tent. The Lord would speak to Moses face to face, as one speaks to a friend. Then Moses would return to the camp, but his young aide Joshua son of Nun did not leave the tent.

Consider This

I've never noticed the first few words in today's text until now, and they trouble my soul. Let me explain.

Now Moses used to take a tent and pitch it outside the camp . . .

The text indicates this is something that Moses used to do, which implies that somewhere along the way he stopped doing it. Did he get too busy? Did the demands of the bigger tent (a.k.a. the tabernacle) consume his time? Did he slowly slip from desperate dependence on God to a manageable comfort level of life? I wonder if he noticed as the folded-up tent collected dust in the corner. It happens so easily as the campfires of pure devotion get replaced by the commercial furnaces of duty or the intolerable urgency of our overscheduled lives and busy agendas.

Why does it trouble me? I used to do this too. You may remember a few weeks back I shared some of the story of my great prayer awakening. In case you missed it, as I was preparing in law school to become the president of the United States (haha!) I also served as the security guard at a local church in town. One night, while making the rounds, I found the front door of the sanctuary ajar. Instead of locking it back up, I ventured inside. In those next few moments, in an ordinary yet profoundly supernatural way, I entered the sanctuary as the house of prayer, or as I have come to understand in retrospect—the house of prayer entered me.

Here's the rest of the story. During rounds the next night, I unlocked the door and let myself in. My experience of prayer seemed to pick up just where I had left off the prior night. Same thing the next night, which became weeks and then months. This sacred space had become my everyday tent of meeting just outside the campgrounds of my everyday life.

As this unfolded, I had also become a volunteer youth worker at the church. My little house next to the church was quickly turning into a hospitality house for the kids in the youth group. As an interesting aside, the house had a sign on the front that said, "The Koinonia House." *Koinonia* is a term

RIGHT HERE. RIGHT NOW.

we see used in the Acts of the Apostles, which means the fellowship of the Holy Spirit.

One night when it came time to make my rounds, a couple of the kids hanging out at the Koinonia House asked if they could go with me. Why not?! As we came to the sanctuary door I had a choice to make. Would I skip my nightly prayer meeting with the Lord or ask them to wait outside or . . . would I invite them to join me? You know what I did. I skipped it. No! I invited them to join me. And from this humble beginning, the awakening grew. Within weeks, more kids began to show up at the Koinonia House in order to join the growing security patrol to make the rounds.

I can still see it in my mind's eye; some nights up to twenty-something kids lined across the altar rail kneeling at the front of that sanctuary. Some nights we would be there for an hour or more meeting with God. At one point, we began to spread out throughout the room, each taking one of the long wooden pews and praying for the people who had sat there the prior Sunday and who would sit there the coming one. Several of the kids approached me later with the idea of camping out in our newfound tent of meeting for an all-night prayer vigil. It was incredible and none of us will ever forget it. And get this—the miracle of awakening began to rise up in the larger church, led by an unlikely band of teenagers who had discovered the power of the Holy Spirit in, of all places, the sanctuary.

And the most beautiful part, to this day many of those kids are still pressing out onto the frontiers of God's kingdom in all sorts of places all over the world. And still to this day, the awakening continues to cut new channels of grace and mercy in that local church and broader community. As I look back, I thank God for leaders then (and now) who tolerated the spilled Dr. Pepper and scattered Nacho Cheese Doritos crumbs left behind from our all-night prayer meetings. They allowed it to blend into the carpet, where I'm sure it still lingers mingled with those teenaged prayers that keep bearing fruit.

I'm pretty sure I don't need to do the translation work here with Moses and his tent of meeting. You've already done it.

The Prayer
Lord Jesus, you are right here, right now. Right here, Jesus. I want a tent of meeting with you. Even more, I want you to take this frail and fragile physical body of mine and make it your tent of meeting with me. Let it become the kind of tent into which you can invite others to join, and one that evokes a holy reverence at the mystery of how divine treasure dwells in the mess of a human life yielded to you. Right here, Jesus. Right now, Jesus. Amen.

The Questions
- Do you have a tent of meeting type story in your past or present life of faith? Consider sharing it with our Facebook group or with your band.
- Are there people in your past or present life whose life of prayer inspires you and causes the worship of God to rise up in you? Reflect on those people. Are they trying to be

those kinds of people or are they just trying to belong to Jesus completely?

- Have the duties or burdens of Christian leadership and responsibility snuffed out the primitive fires of faith that once burned? What might a new tent of meeting practice look like for you?

The Only Distinction That Matters

43

EXODUS 33:15–18 | Then Moses said to [the LORD], "If your Presence does not go with us, do not send us up from here. How will anyone know that you are pleased with me and with your people unless you go with us? What else will distinguish me and your people from all the other people on the face of the earth?"

And the LORD said to Moses, "I will do the very thing you have asked, because I am pleased with you and I know you by name."

Then Moses said, "Now show me your glory."

Consider This

How shall we close these Old Testament readings on prayer and open up our series on prayer and the New Testament?

Let's begin with the piercing question posed by Moses before God:

"What else will distinguish me and your people from all the other people on the face of the earth?"

Moses knew neither he nor the people could distinguish themselves. Essential as they are, it is not our orthodox beliefs that distinguish us. Important as they are, it is not our holy habits that distinguish us. We are distinguished by God's presence alone.

God's presence is known and encountered by those who walk with God in a life of prayer. In yesterday's text we were told, "The Lord would speak to Moses face to face, as one speaks to a friend" (Exod. 33:11).

In today's text, God reassures Moses of his presence with these words, *"I will do the very thing you have asked, because I am pleased with you and I know you by name."*

And if that weren't enough, God granted Moses a glimpse of his glory, hiding him in the cleft of the rock and appearing to him. Moses had a unique, one-of-a-kind relationship with God, but it bears no comparison to the kind of relationship God has opened up for us. Look at how Paul makes the comparison in his second letter to the Corinthians:

> Now if the ministry that brought death, which was engraved in letters on stone, came with glory, so that the Israelites could not look steadily at the face of Moses because of its glory, transitory though it was, will not the ministry of the Spirit be even more glorious? (2 Cor. 3:7–8)

And then in a spectacular turn, reaching all the way back to Genesis 1, Paul drops this: "For God, who said, 'Let light shine out of darkness,' made his light shine in our hearts to give us the light of the knowledge of God's glory displayed in the face of Christ" (2 Cor. 4:6).

Most of us have had a kind of doctrinal conversion. We have believed on the truth of the gospel of Jesus Christ. We have felt our sins forgiven at some level and we do our best to be Christian. I do not want to question the legitimacy of this place of faith. I only want to say there is a much better, richer, deeper, and more alive place of faith.

The only way, really, to get from the former place to the latter is not by denouncing the former place but by becoming discontent with it. It requires an ever-increasing appetite for the presence of God. This quest delves far deeper than the water table of mere religious experience. It is an abandoned seeking after the glory of God displayed in the face of Jesus Christ.

Let me close this first half of the Daily Text series on prayer with a story. Blaise Pascal was a brilliant seventeenth-century scientist, mathematician, philosopher, and later theologian. His faith had been nominal at best until one night as he prepared for bed. He encountered the manifest presence of God in a mystical and supernatural way. He described it as follows:

> The year of grace 1654,
>
> Monday, 23 November, feast of St. Clement, pope and martyr, and others in the martyrology. Vigil of

St. Chrysogonus, martyr, and others. From about half
past ten at night until about half past midnight,
FIRE.

GOD of Abraham, GOD of Isaac, GOD of Jacob
not of the philosophers and of the learned.
Certitude. Certitude. Feeling. Joy. Peace.
GOD of Jesus Christ.
My God and your God.
Your GOD will be my God.
Forgetfulness of the world and of everything,
except GOD.
He is only found by the ways taught in the Gospel.
Grandeur of the human soul.
Righteous Father, the world has not known you, but
I have known you.
Joy, joy, joy, tears of joy.
I have departed from him:
They have forsaken me, the fount of living water.
My God, will you leave me?
Let me not be separated from him forever.
This is eternal life, that they know you, the one true
God, and the one that you sent, Jesus Christ.
Jesus Christ.
Jesus Christ.
I left him; I fled him, renounced, crucified.
Let me never be separated from him.
He is only kept securely by the ways taught in the
Gospel:

Renunciation, total and sweet.

Complete submission to Jesus Christ and to my director.

Eternally in joy for a day's exercise on the earth.

May I not forget your words. Amen.[9]

He later took the piece of paper on which he had written the account and sewed it into the lining of his jacket where it remained undiscovered until his death.

See you in Galilee!

The Prayer

Right here, Jesus. Right now, Jesus. Amen.

The Questions

- What are your Old Testament takeaways as it relates to prayer?
- How has your praying changed as a result of these past several weeks of reading together?
- What is the place of greatest challenge in your life of prayer right now?

9   The document is called Pascal's Memorial. Find it here at http://www.users .csbsju.edu/~eknuth/pascal.html.

PART 2

New Testament Prayers

Welcome to the New Testament of Prayer

44

JOHN 14:12–14 | "Very truly I tell you, whoever believes in me will do the works I have been doing, and they will do even greater things than these, because I am going to the Father. And I will do whatever you ask in my name, so that the Father may be glorified in the Son. You may ask me for anything in my name, and I will do it."

Consider This

While we began the series on prayer with the Old Testament, we chose to begin with the ascension of Jesus Christ. It will also serve as our beginning point for this New Testament prayer series.

Today's text offers a treasure trove of revelation for reflection. Let's focus around these seven words today and come back to the rest of the text later in the series.

"... because I am going to the Father."

Why did the ascension matter so much to the early Christians and so little to us? Over the centuries, the church has tended to place the emphasis on one of two events. Many of us have been involved in the part of the church that centers everything around the Word of God and, more particularly, the death and the resurrection of Jesus Christ. Others of us have participated in the part of the church that centers every-thing around the Day of Pentecost and the coming of the Holy Spirit. Neither side would deny the importance of the other. They focus differently. The challenge comes with the way focus can become overemphasis, and the problem with over-emphasis is that it necessarily creates under-emphasis. Here's the tendency history shows us. Overemphasis on the Word leads to under-emphasis on the Spirit. Overemphasis on the Spirit leads to under-emphasis on the Word.

Our modern sensibilities lead us to seek some kind of balance between the two. The problem with balance is it always leads to tension. These two great verities of our faith, Word and Spirit, do not exist in tension. They live in perfect union, in the person of Jesus Christ.

In Jesus Christ we see what the perfect union of the Word of God and the Spirit of God looks like in a human being. He dwells in the heavenly realm as a human being, in a post-resurrection body, presiding as the Lord of heaven and earth.

Why must we recover the centrality of the ascension of Jesus Christ? Because Jesus Christ is now ascended. It is the present and future reality. His death and resurrection are facts of history. Pentecost and the outpouring of the Holy Spirit is a fact of history. The present state of affairs, which will extend into all eternity is this: Jesus Christ is the Lord of heaven and earth—ruling the cosmos—at the right hand of the throne of God, right here, right now.

So "because I am going to the Father . . ." now what?

"Very truly I tell you, whoever believes in me will do the works I have been doing, and they will do even greater things than these, because I am going to the Father."

Here is where the New Testament of prayer comes into play.

"And I will do whatever you ask in my name, so that the Father may be glorified in the Son. You may ask me for anything in my name, and I will do it."

Go back over those words very slowly, carefully, and with great deliberation. It will be the shaping force of our curriculum going forward.

So did Jesus get it wrong, or have we missed the point?

The Prayer

Almighty, ascended Lord Jesus Christ, you are right here, right now. We hear you say we will do greater things than you, because you go to the Father. Help us understand why we aren't doing those greater things. Teach us, Lord. Right here, Jesus. Right now, Jesus. Amen.

The Questions

- What is your level of understanding and appreciation of the significance of the ascension of Jesus?
- Why do you think we are not doing the greater things Jesus said we would do? Did he get it wrong? Or have we missed the point?
- Have you tended to err on overemphasizing the Word or the Spirit in your faith? Do you see how a restored focus on the ascended Lord Jesus Christ could change things?

45 Is It Time to Re-Presence Your Practice of Prayer?

HEBREWS 10:19–22 | Therefore, brothers and sisters, since we have confidence to enter the Most Holy Place by the blood of Jesus, by a new and living way opened for us through the curtain, that is, his body, and since we have a great priest over the house of God, let us draw near to God with a sincere heart and with the full assurance that faith brings, having our hearts sprinkled to cleanse us from a guilty conscience and having our bodies washed with pure water.

Consider This

Therefore, brothers and sisters, since we have confidence to enter the Most Holy Place . . .

Now there are four words we would never expect to see in the same biblical sentence: *Most Holy Place* and *confidence*. You will remember, the Most Holy Place, also known as, "the Holy of Holies," is the place inside the place inside the place. There was the larger temple and, within that, separated by a curtain, was the Holy Place. And beyond yet another curtain was the Most Holy Place. The ark of the covenant resided here and atop it, the mercy seat—the dwelling place of God on earth.

On one day of the year, the Day of Atonement, a human being, the high priest, would enter the Most Holy Place to sprinkle blood on the mercy seat as an offering of atonement for the people. Tradition has it they stitched bells inside his robe and tied a rope around him so if he fell dead while inside they would hear the bells and be able to pull him out without entering in themselves. This would be the opposite of confidence to enter.

. . . by the blood of Jesus . . .

Because of the blood that Jesus shed on the cross, we have full, immediate, and continuous access to *the* Most Holy Place, which is the dwelling place of God: Father, Son, and Holy Spirit. We get to go inside. It raises a big question, though. Where is the Most Holy Place and how do we get in?

. . . by a new and living way opened for us through the curtain, that is, his body . . .

Remember what happened to the curtain separating the Holy Place from the Most Holy Place in the temple in Jerusalem as Jesus died on the cross? In a stunning miraculous occurrence, it was torn from top to bottom. The old way, through the blood of dead animals, was now replaced by the new and living way; the glorified body of the resurrected Jesus Christ is the new curtain.

The Most Holy Place is now wherever he is. And he is with us, seated in the heavens at the right hand of God, and dwelling by the power of the Holy Spirit in our innermost selves.

. . . and since we have a great priest over the house of God . . .

There's the clear nod to the ascension of Jesus. Now, what do we know about the house of God? The house of God is the house of prayer. This means the Most Holy Place is the most prayer-filled place.

So the Most Holy Place, in a sense, has gone from somewhere very specific to everywhere, which is another way of saying, nowhere in particular. The problem with everywhere is the loss of any sense of place. Everywhere can mean anywhere, and anywhere can easily become nowhere. It happens so easily. When our practice of prayer loses a sense of place, it can also lose a sense of other dimensions, and before we know it, we kind of think of our prayers and our thoughts in the same way. Before we know it, what was once sacred has become casual.

Some will cite Brother Lawrence and his celebrated approach to practicing the presence of God in all things. He famously said that God was as present to him when he washed the dishes as when he was praying in the church. Certainly this is true; however, unmoored from any definitive practices of prayer, this easily drifts in time into a shallow presumption of God's presence and, finally, into spiritual laziness.

What many of us need, both beginners and veterans alike, may not be so much to practice the Presence as to presence our practice. I think Jesus was getting at this when he said, "But when you pray, go into your room, close the door and pray to your Father, who is unseen. Then your Father, who sees what is done in secret, will reward you" (Matt. 6:6).

The Most Holy Place is everywhere, but unless we do the tangible work of locating it somewhere, chances are, for us, it will be nowhere. Because prayer can be so intangible, it needs some tangibility. Do you have such a room as Jesus references? Are there any set times? How about any set prayers?

Let's be clear. There is nothing sacrosanct about your particular place or my particular place other than the way it helps us *"to enter the Most Holy Place by the blood of Jesus, by a new and living way opened for us through the curtain, that is, his body."*

We began our Old Testament series on prayer at stratospheric heights and at impractical depths. This New Testament prayer series begins at ground level with profound practicality. I want you to find or create space for prayer, and not just space but *a* space. This is about giving more presence to our practice. Some of you may already have such a place. If this is you, I want to challenge you to step beyond that familiar comfort zone. I'm not saying change it, but find a way to re-presence your practice.

In my case, I've gotten comfortable sitting in a certain chair on the back porch in the morning. It has become an undefined kind of practice where I easily bounce between the Bible app on my phone in one minute and Gmail the next. In other words, my practice has become un-presenced.

Sometimes finding the Most Holy Place can require creating a more "holy," which is to say "set apart," practice. I think now might be one of those kinds of times for many.

You in?

The Prayer

Almighty, ascended Lord Jesus Christ, you are high and exalted and near as my breath. Teach me this new and living way of drawing near to you with a renewed confidence. Train me to bring my presence into your presence. Right here, Jesus. Right now, Jesus. Amen.

The Questions
- Do you sense that your approach to prayer has fallen into a lackadaisical practice? Why might that be?
- How do you relate to this challenge to re-presence your practice of prayer?
- How might you create set-apart space as Jesus seemed to call for in your practice of prayer?

46 The Most Obvious Most-Neglected Curriculum for Prayer in the History of Prayer

LUKE 11:1 | One day Jesus was praying in a certain place. When he finished, one of his disciples said to him, "Lord, teach us to pray, just as John taught his disciples."

Consider This

I've been seriously trying to learn to pray for more than thirty years now. Several years ago I had a major epiphany. You know what an epiphany is—it's when you finally see what you've been looking at for so long. Here it is: Jesus' life is our school of prayer. God came to earth in the form of a first-century Jewish peasant. He lived out before our very eyes a revolutionary life behind which was an extravagant life of prayer. A good number of those prayers are written down and have survived to the present day.

If I want to learn to pray, doesn't it make perfect sense that I will make those prayers—uttered by God, written down on scrolls, and now reproduced in books (a.k.a. the Bible) of which I personally own no less than twenty-five—my curriculum? That had never occurred to me before. Has it to you? So how many prayers of Jesus would you say we have written down (without counting any twice)? Scholars will surely debate this, but I'm going with nine. I count nine.

For the next several weeks we will work our way through these nine prayers and see what we can learn and how we can grow. Rather than keeping you guessing, here are the nine prayers as I count them:

1. *Matthew 6:9–13.* "Our Father . . ."
2. *Matthew 11:25–26.* "I praise you, Father, Lord of heaven and earth, because you have hidden these things from the wise and learned, and revealed them to little children. Yes, Father, for this is what you were pleased to do."
3. *John 11:41–43.* "Father, I thank you that you have heard me. I knew that you always hear me, but I said this for the benefit of the people standing here, that they may believe that you sent me. . . . Lazarus, come out!"

4. *John 12:27–28.* "Now my heart is troubled, and what shall I say? 'Father, save me from this hour'? No, it was for this very reason I came to this hour. Father, glorify your name!"

5. *Mark 14:36.* "Father, everything is possible. Take this cup from me. Yet not what I will, but what you will."

6. *Luke 23:34.* "Father, forgive them, for they do not know what they are doing."

7. *Mark 15:34.* "*Eloi, Eloi, lama sabachthani?*" ("My God, my God, why have you forsaken me?")

8. *Luke 23:46.* "Father, into your hands I commit my spirit."

9. *John 17:20–21.* "My prayer is not for them alone. I pray also for those who will believe in me through their message, that all of them may be one, Father, just as you are in me and I am in you. May they also be in us so that the world may believe that you have sent me" (see John 17:1–26).

These nine prayers hold an eternity of divine wisdom. Together we will, at minimum, plumb their shallows over the next weeks. As we come into this school of prayer we will be well-served to reorient ourselves with the teacher. And just so you know that I know, I am not the teacher.

One day Jesus was praying in a certain place. When he finished, one of his disciples said to him, "Lord, teach us to pray, just as John taught his disciples."

The Prayer

Almighty, ascended Lord Jesus Christ, you are high and exalted yet near as my breath. We join your ancient disciple in his petition—"Lord, teach us to pray"—only teach us like you taught the Twelve. With the help of the Holy Spirit, we humble ourselves and aspire to be faithful, available, and teachable before you. Right here, Jesus. Right now, Jesus. Amen.

The Questions

- Which of the nine prayers most surprised you to see on the list? Why?
- Have you ever considered these prayers as curriculum in the school of prayer and delved into them as such? Why or why not?
- Faithful, available, and teachable—which is your growing edge? What practical step can you take to mature in that direction?

The Prayer You Probably Never Thought of as a Prayer

47

MATTHEW 11:25–26 | "I praise you, Father, Lord of heaven and earth, because you have hidden these things from the wise and learned, and revealed them to little children. Yes, Father, is what you were pleased to do."

Consider This

Let's begin our nine prayers with one I likely didn't think of before as the kind of prayer one might pray. I call it the "prayer of great reversal."

There's nothing bad about being a wise and learned person—until there is. The minute we think being wise and learned adds anything to our worth as a human being is the minute we bankrupt our sense of worth as a human being. But this is not really about being wise or learned, is it? It's about pride and humility. I love how *The Message* version of the Bible frames todays text: "Abruptly Jesus broke into prayer: 'Thank you, Father, Lord of heaven and earth. You've concealed your ways from sophisticates and know-it-alls, but spelled them out clearly to ordinary people. Yes, Father, that's the way you like to work.'"

Sophisticates and know-it-alls—sounds like pride to me. James, one of Scripture's straightest shooters, quoted from Proverbs when he said, "God opposes the proud but shows favor to the humble" (James 4:6). And if that weren't clear enough, he added, "Humble yourselves before the Lord, and he will lift you up" (James 4:10).

Are you seeing the way the prayer of great reversal works? This prayer opens up a way of reversal in our own spirit and innermost self. It creates the opportunity for a gracious defrocking of our false self—the sense of worth and security we have constructed for ourselves because we were afraid our true selves wouldn't measure up. Grace is never about measuring up. It's the reverse. Grace is about measuring down. God's ways are hidden from the proud and revealed to the humble.

To be clear, pride and humility are not behaviors or even dispositions. Pride and humility come from a much deeper place within—from the depths of our sense of identity. Pride is a telltale sign that a person struggles with shame at the core of their sense of self. They don't mean to be prideful. They can't help it. Shame prevents a person from valuing their own self, which means they must build an alternative sense of self that they can value. Anything that comes against this alternative or false self is vehemently fended off. Pride is a way of protecting the false self. Humility comes from a deep inner sense of knowing you are loved for who you most truly are. This comes from God by the power of his Word and Holy Spirit and through others who have known this kind of unwavering, unconditional love for themselves.

The Message translation continues with these incredible words: Jesus resumed talking to the people, but now tenderly.

> "The Father has given me all these things to do and say. This is a unique Father-Son operation, coming out of Father and Son intimacies and knowledge. No one knows the Son the way the Father does, nor the Father the way the Son does. But I'm not keeping it to myself; I'm ready to go over it line by line with anyone willing to listen." (Matt. 11:27)

Jesus, through his prayer, leads us in the very foundation of prayer, which requires coming before God in simple honesty and true humility. This prayer of reversal, if given a foothold in our prayer life, will chip away at and erode the unstable foundation of our false selves so the true foundation of the unimaginable love of God can be planted. It's why people who have learned to stand on this unshakable foundation are not only people of prayer, they are people of power.

The prayer of great reversal paves the path on the journey from "I am not worthy of love," to "I am loved," to "I am love."

The Prayer
Almighty, ascended Lord, you are high and exalted yet nearer than my breath. I join your prayer as one who wants to come dressed in my impressive wardrobe of my accomplishments while knowing that because these clothes don't fit, they keep me hidden from you. Grant me the courage to be clothed by your grace alone and so become the person you imagined when you created me. Teach me to pray from that graced place. Right here, Jesus. Right now, Jesus. Amen.

The Questions
- What stands out to you about this prayer of great reversal?
- What kind of false self have you constructed as your foundation of worth and security? How have you confused your identity for your accomplishments (or the lack thereof)?
- What would a deeper reversal in your own sense of self before God and others look like in you?

Why the Problem with Over-Confidence and Under-Confidence Are the Same Problem

48

MATTHEW 6:5–8 | "And when you pray, do not be like the hypocrites, for they love to pray standing in the synagogues and on the street corners to be seen by others. Truly I tell you, they have received their reward in full. But when you pray, go into your room, close the door and pray to your Father, who is unseen. Then your Father, who sees what is done in secret, will reward you. And when you pray, do not keep on babbling like pagans, for they think they will be heard because of their many words. Do not be like them, for your Father knows what you need before you ask him."

Consider This

Having covered the prayer of great reversal, which serves as a kind of welcome mat in front of the great house of prayer, we now make a turn to the prayer we commonly know as the Lord's Prayer.

Before proceeding into the prayer itself, we should consider two preliminary matters, the first of which we addressed earlier—the matter of prayer and place. Just as we need to take care not to assume our thoughts are our prayers, we should also be mindful that to say we can pray everywhere can also come to mean that we actually pray nowhere. Place and specific place matters. This is part of the rationale for Jesus telling us to *"go into your room, close the door and pray to your Father, who is unseen."* Note, though the rest of the rationale for this practice:

"And when you pray, do not be like the hypocrites, for they love to pray standing in the synagogues and on the street corners to be seen by others."

This ties back in with yesterday's text about God hiding his ways from the "wise and learned" and revealing them to little children. Remember, pride is all about the projection and management of one's image, which is a way of covering up what is underneath it. Hypocrisy happens when the outer image tells a different story than the inner reality. And the worst kind of pride is religious pride. Real prayer is not for show. "Take it inside," Jesus seems to say.

The second preliminary concern has to do with the form of our praying, and specifically the words. Jesus says the measure of our prayers are not our words.

"And when you pray, do not keep on babbling like pagans, for they think they will be heard because of their many words."

On the one hand, Jesus tells us not to take our cues from the super-pious professionally religious people, and on the other hand he doesn't want us to be misguided by the super-intense uber-wordy methods of the pagans. By pagans, he doesn't necessarily mean the irreligious, but the non-Jewish or Gentile crowd. Insecurity underlies both approaches. The Pharisee turns their lack of intimacy with God to the streets in an effort to prove it to others by keeping up appearances. The pagan turns a lack of intimacy with God into a show of intensity before God as an effort to overcome their insecurity. The Pharisee prays to be seen. The pagan prays to be heard. The Pharisee is plagued by overconfidence in their relationship with God and the pagan by under-confidence.

Here's why this still matters. Within the church, among the followers of Jesus, there still remain both Pharisees and pagans. Am I saying they are not Christians? No, I am not the judge of that. I am saying these ways are alive and well and are traps and pitfalls into which a well-intentioned follower of Jesus can easily fall victim.

This makes Jesus' guidance so critical and helpful to us in what we call, "The Lord's Prayer." He does not give us a form as much as he shows us a format. As we stand on the porch of the house of prayer, the big takeaway from these preliminary teachings has to do with the nature of God and the nature of our relationship with God. Jesus wants us to know the measure of prayer is a secure and intimate relationship with God as Father. It's why overconfidence and under-confidence in our relationship with God turn out to be the same thing. He wants to reassure us before we step into the house of just who we are going to see.

"Then your Father, who sees what is done in secret, will reward you. . . . for your Father knows what you need before you ask him."

Is it any wonder how he will begin to teach us to pray, saying, "Our Father"? To this we will turn next.

The Prayer

Almighty, ascended Lord Jesus Christ, you are high and lifted up and nearer than our breath. Thank you for not only teaching us to pray, but for bringing us into your praying. And thank you for not only bringing us into your praying, but for bringing us into your very relationship with your Father, who you want us to know is our Father too. Right here, Jesus. Right now, Jesus. Amen.

The Questions

- Have you been around Christians who want you to know about their prayer practices, like how early they get up to pray and how long they pray and so forth? Why do we do this?
- Have you been around Christians who seem overly concerned with showing a super-intensity in prayer with words on words on words? Why do we do this?
- Where do you tend to err: on the side of overconfidence in your relationship with God or under-confidence? Why do you think that is?

49 From the Lord's Prayer to the Disciples' Prayer

MATTHEW 6:9–13 | "This, then, is how you should pray: 'Our Father in heaven, hallowed be your name, your kingdom come, your will be done, on earth as it is in heaven. Give us today our daily bread. And forgive us our debts, as we also have forgiven our debtors. And lead us not into temptation, but deliver us from the evil one.'"

Consider This

We come now to perhaps the most-prayed prayer in the history of the world. We know it as "The Lord's Prayer." Roman Catholics call it the "Our Father."

Let's do a high-level overview today and a deeper dive on days following.

Our: The prayer is relational. Though we may be praying this prayer alone in our prayer closet, we never approach God as an individual. *Our* praying is always both personal and communal as opposed to the way we are primarily formed by our Western culture, which is individualized and private. God sees us personally but not outside of our relatedness to others. It's why forgiveness is so critical—coming later in the prayer.

Father: personal. The typical way a Jewish prayer would open was, "Blessed are you, O Lord our God, the King of the universe." Remember, Jesus is not merely teaching us to pray like he prays. He is bringing us into his relationship with "our Father." Father language is not intended to attach gender to God. The word *Father* signifies family, character, or nature and role.

In heaven: presence. Where is God? From the great fall in the garden, God has dwelt in the realm of the heavens. The holiness of God could not abide the presence of our corrupted humanity. It is not because God despised humanity that he departed from our presence in Eden. It was because he loved us. The unadulterated presence of his holiness would have consumed us in our fallenness.

Hallowed be your name: power. It makes sense that "Our Father" would be followed by "hallowed be your name." We must remain mindful that we are on earth and God is in heaven. Though he be our Father, he is holy. Though he be holy and in heaven, we must not assume this means he is distant. Heaven is not somewhere out there. It is the unseen realm just through the veil. It is right here, right now. To say "[holy is] your name" is not to keep our distance, but to retain our reverence. We approach with confidence and in a familial way but not casually and presumptuously.

Your kingdom come: purpose. *Your will be done on earth as it is in heaven*. This is God's great plan. Jesus makes this the first petition. He wants for God's great plan to become our great purpose and guiding priority in all things. Hence we make it the prayer within all our prayers.

Give us today our daily bread: provision. This is code language for, "Remember manna?" Remember how manna worked? Each morning it was provided. They gathered enough for the day's need. On the day prior to Sabbath they gathered enough for two days. Anything gathered beyond what was needed rotted. Bottom line: there will always be scarcity in our hoarding but abundance in God's giving.

And forgive us our debts, as we also have forgiven our debtors: peace. We need to live at peace with others. We begin by taking stock of the debts owed us—our accounts receiv-ables, if you will. Not literal debts but anything done to us, directly or indirectly, intentionally or negligently, offensively or defensively, we need to wipe the slate clean—cancel the foul. Next we take our own sins to God to ask for the same from him for ourselves.

And lead us not into temptation, but deliver us from the evil one: protection. We are far more vulnerable than we realize. The reason we don't realize it is because we spend so much energy trying to protect ourselves. Jesus does not want our energy and resources going into self-protection, rather, he wants us to trust in his protection. Temptation concerns our weakness. Deliverance from evil concerns our exposure.

Seven P's: *personal, presence, power, purpose, provision, peace, protection.*

This is the big framework. Remember, Jesus gave us this prayer because he didn't want us to expend enormous amounts of energy and anxiety on a multitude of words in our prayers. He said God already knows our needs.

So if God already knows, why bring any of it before him? The Lord's Prayer is more about reminding ourselves of our real needs and who can be trusted to meet those needs. It is a prayerful rehearsal of our core faith. This prayer is about building a powerful foundation of confidence in God so that our praying can get out of our closet and take the shape of decisive action in the world.

The Prayer

Almighty, ascended Lord Jesus Christ, you are high and exalted, yet nearer than our breath. Thank you for this prayer of faith. Thank you for making clear to us that the measure of our praying does not consist in making sure we ask for everything, but in a lived faith that you are taking care of everything. Make that a real place for me and not just an ideal. Right here, Jesus. Right now, Jesus. Amen.

The Questions

- What is missing in the Lord's Prayer? Anything you would expect to be in a prayer like this that you don't see?
- How have you engaged the Lord's Prayer in your experience? How has it helped? Hindered?
- What if you could cease particularizing the many and varied things we need that fall underneath these major petitions? What would trusting that God knows our needs without our even asking mean for our life of prayer?

50 How the Lord's Prayer Became an Adventure in Missing the Point

MATTHEW 6:9–13 | "This, then, is how you should pray: 'Our Father in heaven, hallowed be your name, your kingdom come, your will be done, on earth as it is in heaven. Give us today our daily bread. And forgive us our debts, as we also have forgiven our debtors. And lead us not into temptation, but deliver us from the evil one.'"

Consider This

What if our approach to and experience of the Lord's Prayer has largely been an adventure in missing the point? I'm beginning to think so (at least for me). Please don't confuse my boldness in what follows for arrogance. I'm just going to say it and receive what corrections and rebukes may come in return.

We get the Lord's Prayer wrong. For starters, shouldn't it be called, "The Disciples' Prayer"? It is the Lord, after all, to whom we are praying.

Second, Jesus seems to teach the prayer for use in one's prayer closet rather than as a corporate recitation. Could it be our entire misguided experience with the prayer as a public recitation has served to steer us away from engaging the prayer behind closed doors as intended?

Third, I have heard many teachings instructing that Jesus didn't intend us to simply repeat the words of the Lord's (I mean, the Disciples') Prayer. They say, instead, Jesus intended the several petitions to serve as a pattern or guide for our praying; that Jesus intended us to expand our praying within each area. If that's the case, why did Jesus give us the prayer after instructing us to keep the word count down—with the stated reason being, "your Father knows what you need before you ask him" (v. 8)?

If we take the text in its clear and plain sense, we would go into our room, close the door, and pray the fifty-three words that make up the prayer. Why has it never occurred to me to do exactly what Jesus said to do in his abundantly clear instructions? It strikes me as a stunningly simplified, revolutionary approach.

Could Jesus literally mean what he actually said?

I've got a theory on this I will share tomorrow. For now, how about we do an experiment together? For the rest of this series on prayer, including today, let's try doing exactly as Jesus instructed us.

Go into a room. Close the door. Say the fifty-three words aloud to God. Leave. Seriously, leave. Might not hurt to take a knee, but if it does hurt, skip that part.

The Prayer

Almighty, ascended Lord Jesus Christ, you are high and exalted yet nearer than my breath. Thank you for the Disciples' Prayer. Forgive me for missing the point. Come, Holy Spirit, and teach my spirit the simple obedience of following Jesus' plain instructions. Right here, Jesus. Right now, Jesus. Amen.

The Questions

- So what do you think—how is it that we have managed to take a prayer given for personal time with God and turn it into what can so often be a meaningless corporate motion?

- Why do you think we have needed to interpret Jesus' seemingly clear teaching about how to engage the Disciples' Prayer with our own ideas?
- What do you think is the major point of the Disciples' Prayer? Will you join the experiment with us? How about starting right now?

The Problem When Our Problems Consume Our Praying

51

MATTHEW 6:9–13 | "'This, then, is how you should pray: 'Our Father in heaven, hallowed be your name, your kingdom come, your will be done, on earth as it is in heaven. Give us today our daily bread. And forgive us our debts, as we also have forgiven our debtors. And lead us not into temptation, but deliver us from the evil one.'"

Consider This

I remember the first day of class in my freshman year of college. The professor drew a diagram on the board of a pyramid he introduced to us as Maslow's Hierarchy of Needs. He explained Abraham Maslow's theory that human beings start at the lowest and most basic level of needs for physical survival and work their way up to the highest-level need of self-actualization. Here is the hierarchy of needs:

Physical: air, water, food, rest, health, etc.

Security: safety, shelter, stability

Social: belonging, being loved, inclusion, etc.

Ego: self-esteem, power, recognition, prestige

Self-Actualization: finding meaning through larger purpose

In the pyramid scheme it looks like this, in the reverse order with the physical at the bottom and self-actualization at the top.

The fascinating thing about the Lord's Prayer is the way it corresponds with the hierarchy of needs. Watch this:

Physical: *Give us today our daily bread* (provision)

Security: *Lead us not into temptation but deliver us from the evil one* (protection)

Social: *Forgive us our debts, as we also have forgiven our debtors* (peace)

Ego: *Hallowed be your name* (power)

Self-Actualization: *Your kingdom come, your will be done, on earth as it is in heaven* (purpose)

The Lord's Prayer also inverts the pyramid, with the base at the top and the top at the bottom. In other words, we aren't climbing our way up the pyramid through a quest of meeting a hierarchy of needs. We begin at the very bottom with the consuming purpose of God's kingdom and trust our needs to be met by God.

Later in this same chapter, Jesus challenges us not to worry about food and clothes and all the needs of our lives, which can generate so much anxiety and worry. He says instead,

"But seek first his kingdom and his righteousness, and all these things will be given to you as well" (Matt. 6:33).

"All these things," also known as "our problems," fall into the categories of provision, protection, and peace, and can consume every bit of our waking lives. Jesus doesn't want us consumed by our problems but captured by the consuming priority of "your kingdom come, your will be done, on earth as it is in heaven."

That's my theory on why Jesus wants the Disciples' Prayer to be the fifty-three-word extent of lifting up our basic needs before him behind closed doors. He wants the bulk of our time to be spent praying on-location, as we move about the everyday, walking-around world of family, work, and community—in the zone of "your kingdom come, your will be done, on earth as it is in heaven."

In other words, I don't think he wants us to spend a lot of time in our prayer closets praying about our problems (or other people's problems, for that matter). Don't you think that instead of praying in our closets for hungry people to be fed (or fill in any number of other things we might pray about), he would rather us prayerfully go about feeding them?

Summarizing: the problem of our problems is the way they can consume our praying. When Jesus' passion, which is his kingdom, becomes our priority, our problems become his priority.

Am I saying these words should be the extent of our "behind closed doors" praying? No, but for purposes of our

Disciples' Prayer experiment, that's all I am asking us to do in our prayer closets for the next several weeks. Remember the challenge?

Go into a room. Close the door. Say the fifty-three words aloud to God. Leave. Seriously, leave.

I can already tell. This is going to change me.

The Prayer

Almighty, ascended Lord Jesus Christ, you are high and exalted yet nearer than our breath. Bring new order and clear dimension and fresh power to my praying. Show me what a closet prayer looks like and then lead me in how prayer on the streets works. I am ready for your ancient yet new ways. Right here, Jesus. Right now, Jesus. Amen.

The Questions

- Have you accepted the Disciples' Prayer experiment challenge? Why or why not? How is that going?
- What do you think of the way the Lord's Prayer matches up with Maslow's Hierarchy of Needs?
- What do you think about the way the Lord's Prayer inverts the hierarchy into a lowerarchy, where everyone can find and fulfill the big purpose at the bottom level while learning to trust God, rather than having to climb to the top?

The Centrality of "Our Father" in an Age of Gender Confusion

52

MATTHEW 6:9 | "This, then, is how you should pray: 'Our Father in heaven, hallowed be your name.'"

Consider This

Warning label: Today's reading will frustrate some, be off-putting to some, and seem irrelevant to others. Many others will find it instructive in healing ways. One of the great barriers to a life of prayer is our own broken and distorted images of God. Our broken images of God need healing if we are to grow in prayer. I wrote the entry below, posted it, and later retracted it. (Some of you got the post in your e-mail, but most did not.) I think I feared being misunderstood and criticized. I have decided to go ahead and run it.

We all have a Father in heaven. We do not or did not all have a father on earth. We all have a male progenitor to be sure, but not necessarily a father. Many people who did not experience a good father in their childhood understandably have a difficult time approaching and experiencing God as a good Father. Their image of a father is distorted. As a result, when it comes to God, many have rejected the image and language of a father. Some insist father language is a vestige of oppressive patriarchy and press for its eradication.

Here's my question: Instead of allowing a broken father experience on earth to cause rejection of the possibility of experiencing a good Father in heaven, why don't we allow for the possibility of a good Father in heaven to heal our memory of a broken father on earth?

I recognize the complex difficulties and often atrocious histories here, and I have no right to instruct anyone in their experience of God. I am attempting to offer pastoral wisdom. Some respond by noting the many rich ways to know God's nature other than Father, even noting God's motherly qualities. True enough, however, the biblical prominence of Father language for God, most notably from Jesus, points to something essential and irreplaceable about the Fatherhood of God as a core tenet of the Christian faith.

To the extent we misunderstand the nature of God we will misappropriate the nature of humanity. The present-day confusion around human gender is a case in point.

As confusion around gender identity grows, our clarity around the personhood and nature of God must increase all the more. We must remember when we talk about God we are not speaking in the categories of biology and gender but rather about theology and spirituality—the realm of Spirit and truth. God has no gender. To call God Father does not mean God is in any way male any more than to call God mother would assign God to a feminine gender. Fatherhood, and for that matter, motherhood, are not so much biological categories as they are spiritual realities. They are spiritual identities exercised through spiritual practices.

Some may be scratching their heads at this point, wondering why I have chosen to wade into these waters today and what this has to do with the Disciples' Prayer. We live in a day of unprecedented confusion when it comes to human gender. It creates barriers to prayer.

As gender confusion increases, the state of human community divides and decreases. The way to community will not come through sociological or political theory but from theological clarity. The foundation of theological clarity begins with the Word of God, revealed by Jesus, the Son of God, through the inspiration of the Spirit of God.

So what does all of this have to do with prayer and, more specifically, the Disciples' Prayer? Everything. After all, when Jesus taught us to pray he revealed our starting place with two words. They are the two most game-changing words of Jesus: "Our Father."

The Prayer

Almighty, ascended Lord Jesus Christ, you are high and exalted yet nearer than our breath. We need your mind to gain clarity amid so much confusion in our culture and world today. Sort our confusion in your school of prayer and give us great patience. Right here, Jesus. Right now, Jesus. Amen.

The Questions

- Do you see how our broken sense of God's image can hinder our praying?

- None of us had perfect parents. How does your experience of your parents growing up impact your present-day experience with God, for better and for worse?
- What shape has the healing of your own image of who God is and what God is like taken in your life?

53 A Few More Words on Letting Our Words Be Few

MATTHEW 6:9 | "This, then, is how you should pray: 'Our Father in heaven, hallowed be your name.'"

Consider This

"Hallowed be your name."

This would be the opposite of "taking the Lord's name in vain."

To hallow, which means to set apart and make holy, is an act of worship. It does not mean to formalize but to reverence. Formalizing has the effect of creating distance. Reverencing has the effect of drawing near without presumption. Consider Isaiah's vision in chapter 6:

> In the year that King Uzziah died, I saw the Lord, high and exalted, seated on a throne; and the train of his robe filled the temple. Above him were seraphim, each with six wings: With two wings they covered their

faces, with two they covered their feet, and with two they were flying. And they were calling to one another: "Holy, holy, holy is the LORD Almighty; the whole earth is full of his glory."

At the sound of their voices the doorposts and thresholds shook and the temple was filled with smoke. (vv. 1–4)

It reminds me also of the text in Ecclesiastes: "Do not be quick with your mouth, do not be hasty in your heart to utter anything before God. God is in heaven and you are on earth, so let your words be few" (5:2).

In that spirit . . . enough said.

The Prayer

Almighty, ascended Lord Jesus Christ, you are high and exalted yet nearer than our breath. Holy! Holy! Holy! Hallowed be thy name. Right here, Jesus. Right now, Jesus. Amen.

The Questions

No further questions.

Why There Is Only One Prayer

54

MARK 1:14–15 | After John was put in prison, Jesus went into Galilee, proclaiming the good news of God. "The time has come," he said. "The kingdom of God has come near. Repent and believe the good news!"

Consider This

The Disciples' Prayer offers remarkable wisdom for a life of prayer. Provision and protection are two areas of concern that threaten to consume our prayer bandwidth, holding us in the gravity of our own fears. Jesus does not want us filling our prayers with temporal concerns for ourselves or for others. In fact, rather than praying for the basic temporal needs of others, he would prefer that we just met those needs. I would cite Matthew 25 and the parable of the sheep and the goats in support.

The point of our Great Prayer Closet Fifty-Three-Word Challenge is not to reduce our prayer time, but to shift the *way* we spend our time in prayer. Whether in the prayer closet or not, Jesus gives us a singular priority: the kingdom of God advancing on earth as it is in heaven. The kingdom of God is the movement. When we pray for awakening, we are praying for the advance of the kingdom of God.

Jesus' first message, his driving ambition, his dying declaration, his resurrection power and the agenda of his ascended rule, all come together in the now-coming kingdom of God. The major shift we must make in our praying is from desperate pleadings to emboldened declaration.

After John was put in prison, Jesus went into Galilee, proclaiming the good news of God. "The time has come," he said. "The kingdom of God has come near. Repent and believe the good news!"

The good news of God is this: the time has come. The kingdom of God has come near.

If we believe this good news, we will repent. Our praying will change. Instead of seeing our prayers as preceding God's next action, we will understand our prayers as proceeding from God's prior activity. Repentance will look like the realignment of our confidence, imagination, and expectation.

Let's be clear. The kingdom of God will not finally come on earth as it is in heaven until Jesus returns and brings it in all its fullness. But to be sure—the good news of God is this: the time has come. The kingdom of God has come near.

This good news represents a dramatic, dynamic shift in what is now possible. Awakening means waking up and rising into the new and now possibility of "on earth as it is in heaven." A great awakening means multitudes waking up and rising into it.

If it is this easy, why are we missing it? It is not enough to simply believe and even to shift the way we pray. We miss the possibility of the kingdom because we misunderstand the nature of repentance. We think of repentance in the thin categories of morality and behavior, which ironically turn out to be self-oriented.

Repentance, in the tradition of the kingdom of God, means to become self-forgetful. We do not become self-forgetful until we become others-focused; until our hearts and minds become gloriously reoriented around the love of God and neighbor. This kind of love, which is the holy convergence of purity and power, is the kingdom of God, on earth as it is in heaven. To repent and believe the good news is the lifelong journey of becoming the love of God in the world—a right here, right now person who carries the phenomenal possibility of a right here, right now God.

More on this tomorrow.

The Prayer

Almighty, ascended Lord Jesus Christ, you are high and exalted yet nearer than our breath. I want to repent and believe the good news of all you have made possible. More than that, I want to become the kind of person you can trust with all of this possibility. I want for my life to realize the possibility of your love in the world. Right here, Jesus. Right now, Jesus. Amen.

The Questions

- How do you relate to this claim from today's reading: "Instead of seeing our prayers as preceding God's next action, we will understand our prayers as proceeding from God's prior activity"?
- What do you think about the shifting of our praying from desperate pleadings to emboldened declarations?
- In your judgment, what does love have to do with it all? Do you see how we get sidetracked in quests for purity on the one hand and power on the other? How does love capture and complete the convergence of purity and power?

The Thing We Need More than Faithfulness in Prayer

55

LUKE 4:16–21 | He went to Nazareth, where he had been brought up, and on the Sabbath day he went into the synagogue, as was his custom. He stood up to read, and the scroll of the prophet Isaiah was handed to him. Unrolling it, he found the place where it is written:

"The Spirit of the Lord is on me, because he has anointed me to proclaim good news to the poor. He has sent me to proclaim freedom for the prisoners and recovery of sight for the blind, to set the oppressed free, to proclaim the year of the Lord's favor."

Then he rolled up the scroll, gave it back to the attendant and sat down. The eyes of everyone in the synagogue were fastened on him. He began by saying to them, "Today this scripture is fulfilled in your hearing."

Consider This

Though twenty years have passed, I remember it like it was yesterday. There I stood in the synagogue in Nazareth, the very same place where Jesus unrolled the scroll and read this celebrated prophecy of Isaiah. Somehow the nod came to me to read this text from Luke's gospel aloud. As I came to the end of the text, I believe the Spirit overcame me. I increased my volume by several levels and began to repeat the last line over and over again,

"Today this scripture is fulfilled in your hearing."

"Today this scripture is fulfilled in your hearing."

"Today this scripture is fulfilled in your hearing."

The audacity of this carpenter's son!

What he said in Mark's gospel in general he says in Luke's gospel with particularity: "The time has come," he said. "The kingdom of God has come near. Repent and believe the good news!" (Mark 1:15).

Luke 4:18–19 describes what it looks like when, "on earth as it is in heaven," happens. The poor hear good news. Prisoners hear word of their freedom. The blind recover their sight. The oppressed are set free. The year of the Lord's favor is announced.

The kingdom of God means the reversal of misfortune, the righting of injustice, the recovery of wellness, the release of flourishing, and the renewal of all things broken. This is power all right, but it is power of a particular nature. There is a word to describe the nature of this kind of power. The word is *love*—not a soft, fluffy, sentimental feeling kind of love but a hard, strenuous, stretching, active kind of love.

This kind of love is not born in the streets through political activism or do-good-ism activity. This love is of another order. It is born from on high into the hearts, minds, and bodies of those who will get low enough to the ground to join that place of sacred intercession where the groaning of the broken creation mingles with the groaning of the Holy

Spirit. Through this kind of praying, the very kingdom of God is sown like seeds in the fertile soil of our broken hearts and across the tortured landscape of our broken world.

"Your kingdom come, your will be done, on earth as it is in heaven" (Matt. 6:10).

This is the heart prayer of the heart of God which longs to be particularized through the love-laden travailing prayers of God's people. In my judgment, this is how the Lord would have us spend the bulk of our time in prayer. One percent of the time on our provision and protection, and 99 percent of the time sowing "kingdom come" from here to there—in this situation and that one.

What we need in our praying, more than earnestness or sincerity or even tears, is the audacity of the love of God— the audacity of a so-called carpenter's son to step out of the familiar expectations of everybody who knew him and to boldly declare,

"Today this scripture is fulfilled in your hearing."

"Today this scripture is fulfilled in your hearing."

"Today this scripture is fulfilled in your hearing."

The thing we need more than faithfulness in prayer is audacity in love.

The Prayer

Almighty, ascended Lord Jesus Christ, you are high and exalted yet nearer than our breath. I want to sign on to your prayer, "Your kingdom come, your will be done, on earth as it is in heaven." Birth those words in me from a place of love, which is the place where your power turns everything around. Right here, Jesus. Right now, Jesus. Amen.

The Questions

- Why does the whole concept of "love" get such bad wrap?
- How might we reclaim the big, biblical God-sized concept of love—holy love?
- What will it take for you to "get low enough to the ground to join that place of sacred intercession where the groaning of the broken creation mingles with the groaning of the Holy Spirit"? It will take more love, right? Holy love!

56 | The Secret behind the Great Power of Prayer

1 CORINTHIANS 13:13 | And now these three remain: faith, hope and love. But the greatest of these is love.

Consider This

We began the New Testament series on prayer with Jesus' word to his disciples: "Very truly I tell you, whoever believes in me will do the works I have been doing, and they will do even greater things than these, because I am going to the Father" (John 14:12).

Why is this not proving true in our experience? I have a working theory. To track it out we need to go to the tomb of Lazarus and explore another of Jesus' nine prayers.

At the tomb of Lazarus, we see the greatest reversal in the kingdom of God—from death to life. You may remember, Lazarus lay in the sealed tomb for four days. Jesus arrived intentionally late knowing this would be the scene of his greatest miracle. Here is the prayer as recorded by John the apostle:

> "Father, I thank you that you have heard me. I knew that you always hear me, but I said this for the benefit of the people standing here, that they may believe that you sent me." When he had said this, Jesus called in a loud voice, "Lazarus, come out!" (John 11:41–43)

And in case you don't know the rest of the story, here it is: "The dead man came out, his hands and feet wrapped with strips of linen, and a cloth around his face" (v. 44).

Did Jesus intend for us to pray prayers like this and see these kinds of outcomes in response? If your answer is no, what do you do with John 14:12 and Jesus' promise of our doing greater things than he did? If your answer is yes, how do you explain our poor performance?

Backing up a step, do we believe Jesus can still raise the dead? If so, why would we not believe the followers of Jesus could raise the dead through prayer in Jesus' name? How else do we suppose it might happen?

It is happening in other parts of the world; just not so much where we live. Why not? My theory: we are asleep to the greater works of God because we have an anemic concept of the greater love of God.

Take a look at this series of verses surrounding the Lazarus story and note in particular the nature of Jesus' love for this family.

"So the sisters sent word to Jesus, 'Lord, the one you love is sick'" (v. 3).

"Now Jesus loved Martha and her sister and Lazarus" (v. 5).

"When Jesus saw her weeping, and the Jews who had come along with her also weeping, he was deeply moved in spirit and troubled" (v. 33).

"Jesus wept" (v. 35).

"Then the Jews said, 'See how he loved him!'" (v. 36).

"Jesus, once more deeply moved, came to the tomb. It was a cave with a stone laid across the entrance. 'Take away the stone,' he said" (vv. 38–39).

Don't you think the way these relationships are described is more than a little bit extraordinary? The story continues with Jesus' question.

"Then Jesus said, 'Did I not tell you that if you believe, you will see the glory of God?'" (v. 40).

There is the challenge of faith, which I admittedly struggle with on this matter of raising the dead. This story reveals a far greater challenge than faith. It is the challenge of love. It is one thing to possess faith and quite another to be possessed by divine love. The famous wedding text makes this abundantly clear: "and if I have a faith that can move mountains, but do not have love, I am nothing" (1 Cor. 13:2).

Love is greater than faith, and until our love is greater than our faith, we are destined for far lesser things than the greater things Jesus promised we would do. The great secret behind the great power of prayer is the power of great love.

I realize all of this may seem utterly absurd and impractical to many of you. I will admit, this is not a conventional series on prayer. But what if our conventions have become the problem? What if we have allowed the whole idea of prayer to become so casual and so domesticated by our twenty-first-century first-world problems it is now a caricature of Jesus' intentions?

My friends, prayer moves us into the sacred and powerful domain of divine love, where the supernatural reversals of the kingdom of God are meant to be the rule, rather than the exception. There is too much at stake to try and dial this back to a milk-and-cookies approach.

It is here we come up against the deepest challenge of our discipleship. It is not the challenge of being more disciplined or committed or even faithful. Our greatest challenge lives at the level of our love-less-ness, which is the place of our un-blessed brokenness. Do not despair, though, for Jesus wills to lead us through our brokenness to his brokenness, which becomes the place of blessedness—a place of beautiful scars. We know this place by its sign: the cross.

It is to the prayers of the cross we turn next.

The Prayer

Almighty, ascended Lord Jesus Christ, you are high and exalted yet nearer than our breath. Thank you for raising Lazarus and for opening up the depths of your heart for him and his family for all of us to see. I confess: this kind of love is foreign to my experience. Open me up to this kind of love that holds the power to raise the dead. Right here, Jesus. Right now, Jesus. Amen.

The Questions

- Do you believe it is even possible to raise the dead through prayer in Jesus' name? Not just theoretically but practically?
- What do you make of this statement: "Love is greater than faith, and until our love is greater than our faith, we are destined for far lesser things than the greater things Jesus promised we would do"?
- What will it take to move from a casual and domesticated prayer life to an awakened life of prayer—whose capacity mirrors the capacities of Jesus himself?

57 | The First Prayer of the Cross: The Prayer for Glory, Part One

JOHN 12:23–28 | Jesus replied, "The hour has come for the Son of Man to be glorified. Very truly I tell you, unless a kernel of wheat falls to the ground and dies, it remains only a single seed. But if it dies, it produces many seeds. Anyone who loves their life will lose it, while anyone who hates their life in this world will keep it for eternal life. Whoever serves me must follow me; and where I am, my servant also will be. My Father will honor the one who serves me.

"Now my soul is troubled, and what shall I say? 'Father, save me from this hour'? No, it was for this very reason I came to this hour. Father, glorify your name!"

Then a voice came from heaven, "I have glorified it, and will glorify it again."

Consider This

We come now to the prayers of the cross. There is a sense in which we should consider all of Jesus' prayers as prayers of the cross. The cross is far more than a day in the life of Jesus. The cross is the totality of the mind of Christ, the redemptive vision of the love of God, and the way of flourishing abundant life marked out for us. The cross is the prosperous way of the kingdom of God, the way "in heaven" becomes embodied "on earth."

The cross is the mysterious secret to the life of prayer envisioned for us by Jesus. We will only find this way by following him, which is why delving into his prayers is so important. His prayers reveal his mind, heart, and vision. Before going further, let's remind ourselves, we aren't in search of tips and tricks to help with our praying. There are technical or surface-level changes, and then there is deep transformation.

This whole study has been about deep transformation and digging the kind of well it takes to sustain a life of prayer. Changes to one's prayer practices can help one grow, like changes to one's diet can help one lose weight, but we all know the problem with dieting: it's technical change rather than deep transformation.

Speaking of dieting, there's an interesting three-letter word tucked into the larger word. Did you catch it? It's also tucked into today's text.

"Very truly I tell you, unless a kernel of wheat falls to the ground and dies, it remains only a single seed. But if it dies, it produces many seeds."

We live in an age where the cross has been reduced to the gateway from earth to heaven. In other words, because of my belief in Jesus' death and resurrection, I get to go to heaven when I die. I'm not saying that's not true. I am saying it's not the biblical vision of the Christian faith. The biblical vision of the Christian faith sees the cross as the gateway from heaven to earth. The cross opens and unfolds the way of "your kingdom come, your will be done, on earth as it is in heaven."

To be clear, the gospel does mean eternal life, and, yes, this comes after death. Here's the massive, beyond-quantum innovation of the gospel: die to live—not later, but now. Many follow Jesus to the cross where they gladly or glibly receive an assurance of eternal life after death. Few follow him through the cross where they find the reality of eternal life now. The secret to life, according to Jesus, is to die before you die.

"Anyone who loves their life will lose it, while anyone who hates their life in this world will keep it for eternal life."

To love one's life means to cling to and pursue one's self-interest, preservation, security, comfort, leisure, luxury, and all the other markers of a worldly prosperity only money can buy. (As an interesting and ironic aside, people often characterize heaven by the size of one's mansion there. Taking a step further, the controlling vision of prosperity looks like a second home for the rich and a lottery ticket for the poor. And because I know I just stepped in it with some readers, the problem is not the second home, it's the lack of vision for it.) To hate one's life means to exchange these things for an interest beyond self, thriving beyond preservation, security beyond wealth, rest beyond leisure, comfort beyond luxury, purpose beyond problem-free life, and, yes, a love beyond power as previously imagined.

"Whoever serves me must follow me; and where I am, my servant also will be. My Father will honor the one who serves me."

This way of the cross is the life of prayer we speak of, and far from a method, it can only be found through the kind of pursuit of Jesus that leads one to abandon every other ambition. It will not make you a fanatic. It will set you free.

Now to the prayer. Let's call this first prayer of the cross the Glory Prayer.

"Now my soul is troubled, and what shall I say? 'Father, save me from this hour'? No, it was for this very reason I came to this hour. Father, glorify your name!"

It took longer to get here than I thought. We will drink together from the well of this prayer tomorrow.

The Prayer

Almighty, ascended Lord Jesus Christ, you are high and exalted yet nearer than our breath. Thank you for revealing your own inner struggle, the trouble of your own soul, the challenge of your life, and the way you prayed your way through. "Father, glorify your name!" Right here, Jesus. Right now, Jesus. Amen.

The Questions

- What do you make of this switch from the cross as the way from earth to heaven to the cross as the way from heaven to earth?
- Have you come to the cross and received Jesus' gift of forgiveness? Are you on the path of coming through the cross and receiving Jesus' gift of freedom?
- What is your primary vision of prosperity? Is it more shaped by the world around you or by the coming kingdom of God? What might help that shift?

The First Prayer of the Cross: The Prayer for Glory, Part Two

58

JOHN 12:27–28 | "Now my soul is troubled, and what shall I say? 'Father, save me from this hour'? No, it was for this very reason I came to this hour. Father, glorify your name!"

Consider This

There is *the* cross, and then there is *my* cross and, finally, there are *our* crosses.

So what is the cross? We could define it as an incredibly shameful form of public execution whereby a notorious criminal is beaten to within an inch of their life, stripped naked, and affixed to two intersecting planks of wood where they are hung suspended until their death by asphyxiation. It would be an accurate depiction of crucifixion but an inadequate definition of the cross.

The cross is the will of God from before the foundation of the world to take the most unjust, inhumane, cruel, and undeserved punishment known to human history and bring from it the most unbelievable, incredible, crowning act of redeeming love known to history and eternity.

"Now my soul is troubled, and what shall I say? 'Father, save me from this hour'? No, it was for this very reason I came to this hour. Father, glorify your name!"

And let's be clear once more. The cross, though finally and fully enacted on a certain Friday outside the gates of the city of Jerusalem around the year thirty-three, is far more than a day in the history of the world. The cross is the comprehensive scope of the preexistent, uncreated second person of the Trinity, who in the fullness of time was conceived by the Holy Spirit and born of the virgin Mary. The cross is etched into the manger at his birth. The cross is sketched into his every day, every deed, every divine act of human compassion, every message, every miracle, even the most mundane movement of his blessed feet across the face of this broken ground. And with every step, the very beat of his heart, the fixation of his mind, the Spirit embedded and embodied this prayer:

"Father, glorify your name!"

The cross is born out through his temptations and trials, according to his prayers, in his friendships, despite his enemies, by his discipleship, in light of betrayals and denials and abandonment. The cross is weighted with every rejection, indignity, scornful glance, and whispered accusation, and with every unlikely embrace by every undignified outcast leper, tree-climbing tax collector, and woman of ill repute. The cross is his burial in the borrowed grave of a rich Pharisee. By the cross he descended into death and hell with the gospel of the life of heaven. And most of all, the cross, in the most stunning surprise of human history, enacted the great reversal, swallowing up death by death, as on the third day he arose from the dead!

"Father, glorify your name!"

If you are a regular reader of the Daily Text, you know it doesn't stop here. The cross is engraved on his hands and head and feet in the glorious scars he showed us in those forty days of fellowship following his resurrection when he taught us lessons of the kingdom we could only learn from a risen God. By the cross, he ascended into heaven, sits at the right hand of God, and ever lives to make intercession for the cross to wind its way down every highway and byway, through every alley of every forgotten slum, and through every door of every home of every gated suburban enclave.

"Father, glorify your name!"

The cross was, and is, and ever shall be the atoning sacrifice of the Son of God for the salvation of all of creation. It is salvation from the penalty of sin, deliverance from the power of sin, and restoration from the curse of sin. By this act of utterly inglorious divine love, God finally, fully, and demonstrably revealed his heart, mind, and will for the human race.

And the cross will stand for all eternity, as Jesus triumphantly returns to consummate the kingdom of heaven on earth in all its glorious splendor. In the heart of the heart of God, at the center of the cosmos for all time and eternity stands the Lamb slain from before the foundation of the world. This, my friends, is the cross.

"Father, glorify your name!"

In the largest way and with the fewest words, the cross is the weight of the glory of the love of God for the whole world, beginning with me.

"Father, glorify your name!"

Yes, I said, beginning with me. Why? Because unless the cross begins with me it is never effective for me, and if the cross is never effective for me, it—the weight of the glory of the love of God for the whole world—will never happen through me.

Tomorrow we will make the seamless, yet thorny transition from *the* cross to *my* cross and on to *our* crosses. It is enough today to marvel at the glory of it all in and of itself.

The Prayer

Almighty, ascended Lord Jesus Christ, you are high and exalted yet nearer than our breath. Give me the grace to survey the cross. I confess I so easily reduce the eternal weight of the glory of the love of God to a transaction or a tenet of faith, like a tick box on a software agreement. Teach me to wrestle with it until I revel in it and finally rest in it. Father, glorify your name. Right here, Jesus. Right now, Jesus. Amen.

The Questions

- How do you react/respond to this statement: "The cross is the weight of the glory of the love of God for the whole world, beginning with me"?
- Has the cross tended to be for you a single event on a single day in history, a kind of ledger transaction that you acknowledge and accept on your behalf and then move on?
- What do you make of this press I am making for a much larger grasping of the cross and what implications does it have for your life and discipleship?

The First Prayer of the Cross: the Prayer for Glory, Part Three

59

JOHN 12:27–28 | "Now my soul is troubled, and what shall I say? 'Father, save me from this hour'? No, it was for this very reason I came to this hour. Father, glorify your name!"

Consider This

Let's begin by remembering our framework: *the* cross, *my* cross, *our* crosses.

While we are at it, let's also remember this statement from yesterday's reading: "The cross is the weight of the glory of the love of God for the whole world, beginning with me." This is why the first prayer of the cross is so important:

"Father, glorify your name!"

So, what is *my* cross? It is the weight of the glory of the love of God for me. I like the way Galatians 2:20 expresses it: "I have been crucified with Christ and I no longer live, but Christ lives in me. The life I now live in the body, I live by faith in the Son of God, who loved me and gave himself for me."

My sin is crucified with Christ. I am forgiven, cleansed, and pardoned. It is as if I never sinned. This can be easier to believe than to actually receive. Why? Because along with letting go of our sin, we must also let go of our righteousness. My sin is all the ways I destroy my sense of worth as

215

a human being. My righteousness is all the ways I try and recover that sense of worth. Just as our failures are no longer a mark against us, so our successes are no longer a mark in our favor. Our entire system of ledger-keeping must die.

When the cross becomes *my* cross, I live in the economy of grace, free of the system of condemnation and commendation. I live under the weight of the glory of the unconditional, unmerited, unwavering love of God—which to experience is to truly live.

Here's the kicker: because Jesus carried the weight of the cross, we experience the weightlessness of it. When we can finally let go of all our disqualifications (which is easier), and lay down all our qualifications (which is much harder), we can finally experience being embraced for who we most deeply and truly are. There's more. We can finally set others free from the prison of our condemnation and commendation and embrace them for who they most deeply and truly are. To the extent we live in the system of condemnation and commendation we impose that on others.

The cross becomes *my* cross when I take up my cross and follow Jesus, which means seeking first the kingdom of God and his righteousness and leaving behind the kingdom of the world. Here there is no guilt or shame, no condemnation or commendation. Again, Paul's word to the Galatians captures it: "May I never boast except in the cross of our Lord Jesus Christ, through which the world has been crucified to me, and I to the world" (Gal. 6:14).

Finally, there are *our* crosses. Our crosses come to us in those places where the ways of the kingdom clash with the ways of the world and call on us to make difficult decisions. They usually involve profound surrender of our self-interest and often come at great personal cost. Once the cross becomes my cross, our little crosses (great and small) become the proving grounds where we learn the ways of descent, death, resurrection, and ascension. In this way, this first prayer of the cross becomes actualized in our lives as our Father brings great glory to his name.

These little crosses become the everyday opportunities to lift up the prayer for glory, beginning with an honest assessment of the challenge: *"Now my soul is troubled."*

Realizing the real decision facing us: *"and what shall I say? 'Father, save me from this hour'?"*

Remembering who we are and why we are here: *"No, it was for this very reason I came to this hour."*

And abandoning oneself to the mystery—claiming the cross as my cross in an act of absolute trust, declaring: *"Father, glorify your name!"*

This is the agonizing and astonishing pathway whereby we are transformed from one degree of glory to the next.

Once again from the top, this time with feeling: *"Now my soul is troubled, and what shall I say? 'Father, save me from this hour'? No, it was for this very reason I came to this hour. Father, glorify your name!"*

The Prayer

Almighty, ascended Lord Jesus Christ, you are high and exalted yet nearer than our breath. You are the way of the cross. Lead me ever deeper into this way of making your cross my cross so that my many little crosses become places for the demonstration of your glory. Right here, Jesus. Right now, Jesus. Amen.

The Questions

- Are these connections and progressions clear to you—from the cross to my cross to our crosses? Where does it remain unclear?
- Are you still caught up in the world's ways of conforming us into its pattern through the system of condemnation and commendation? Do you want to be free from it?
- Are you ready to let go of all of your disqualifications to live fully in the kingdom of God? More to the point, are you ready to let go of all your qualifications?

60 The Second Prayer of the Cross: The Gethsemane Prayer

MARK 14:32–38 | They went to a place called Gethsemane, and Jesus said to his disciples, "Sit here while I pray." He took Peter, James and John along with him, and he began to be deeply distressed and troubled. "My soul is overwhelmed with sorrow to the point of death," he said to them. "Stay here and keep watch."

Going a little farther, he fell to the ground and prayed that if possible the hour might pass from him. "*Abba*, Father," he said, "everything is possible for you. Take this cup from me. Yet not what I will, but what you will."

Then he returned to his disciples and found them sleeping. "Simon," he said to Peter, "are you asleep? Couldn't you keep watch for one hour? Watch and pray so that you will not fall into temptation. The spirit is willing, but the flesh is weak."

Consider This

We come to the second prayer of the cross. As we approach, let us remember we want to learn these prayers not from the outside looking in, but from the inside looking out. It is not enough that Jesus is the way and the truth and the life. He must become our way and our truth and our life. If we are to have the same mind in us that was in Christ Jesus, we will discover his mind on prayer through his prayers.

Today we turn to the second great prayer of the cross, which we will call the Gethsemane Prayer. Gethsemane, as you know, is the place Jesus frequently visited with his disciples as a sanctuary place of prayer. It is located on the Mount of Olives just across the Kidron Valley from the walled city of Jerusalem. It was and is to this day a grove of ancient olive trees. It is often referred to as the garden of Gethsemane.

The original fall into temptation and disobedience occurred in a garden. It is no coincidence that Jesus resisted the final temptation and demonstrated the ultimate obedience in another garden. It is fitting that the name "Gethsemane" means "oil press." Jesus faced the unimaginable press of freely submitting to the gravest and most incomprehensible injustice the world has ever witnessed. We see it in the Prayer of Gethsemane.

"Abba, *Father,*" he said, "*everything is possible for you. Take this cup from me. Yet not what I will, but what you will.*"

Note the way he begins, "*Abba*, Father." To speak this name is to enter the house of prayer. It is a term of endearment and intimacy. My children are getting older at twelve, fourteen, sixteen, and eighteen. The younger three still frequently and affectionately call me DaDa. Something about that touches my heart at a depth beyond sentiment. Somewhere along the way we tend to stop using that kind of language that came naturally and even instinctively to us as young children. Most of us were never taught or discipled to draw on this kind of language and imagery when it came to our relationship with God. Jesus uses it consistently and because he wants for us to share his relationship with God, we would be well-served to use this kind of language too.

Next he makes the declaration we see on the lips of saints throughout Scripture from Abraham to Jeremiah to Mary: "*everything is possible for you.*" It is one thing to claim this as an affirmation of faith, as in, "Nothing is impossible with God." It goes to the next level when we make it a personal

declaration to God in prayer: *"everything is possible for you."*
It is more common to hear people lift up their hopes in their
prayers. Jesus begins by lifting up his faith.

Now watch where he goes next. *"Take this cup from me."*
He lifts up his hope to God. Jesus feels enormous anxiety,
isolation, and despair on this night. He knows what has been
set in place. He understands his mission. He knows there will
be resurrection on the other side of death. But still, he is a
human being. He shows us, particularly in the facing of our
little crosses, that it is okay to ask for a pass. It's understand-
able we would want to opt out of suffering even when it is
for a greater good. The fact that we would want to escape
it makes an ultimate decision to endure it all the more
powerful. Beware of the person who wants to suffer. Jesus
hopes something can change. He prays his hope.

He starts with faith, shifts to hope, and now you see where
this is going. *"Yet not what I will, but what you will."* Love.
Jesus prays his love in an act of utter surrender and ultimate
trust. Love is not resignation to a foregone conclusion. Love
means a trusting surrender of one's life to God, over and over
and over and over. Though trust deepens, it never gets easier,
because there always seems to be more at stake to lose. Jesus
makes the conscious decision not to trust in his human
hopes but in divine love.

And let's not miss the renunciation in the prayer. In the
Disciples' Prayer, we train our hearts to beat to the rhythm
of the prayer, "Your kingdom come. Your will be done." Jesus
takes it a step further here by renouncing his will.

"Yet not what I will. . ."

Again, it is one thing to make the claim, "I want to do God's will and not my own will." It is quite another to renounce one's will speaking directly to God in prayer, "Yet not what I will." Note also the difference between this and the tepid prayer of, "If it is your will to (fill in the blank), then please do (fill in the blank)."

This Gethsemane Prayer is a powerful prayer of the cross. It will lead us in the way of Jesus every single time, beginning with faith, moving to hope, and landing on love.

Once more from the top; and this time . . . you know the drill: "Abba, *Father,*" *he said,* "*everything is possible for you. Take this cup from me. Yet not what I will, but what you will.*"

The Prayer

Almighty, ascended Lord Jesus Christ, you are high and exalted yet nearer than our breath. Though you are God, you showed us what it looks like to be fully human in the face of unimaginable difficulty. Thank you for your bold faith, your vulnerable hope, and your trusting love. Train my mind and heart in this way of your cross. Right here, Jesus. Right now, Jesus. Amen.

The Questions

- Does it make you uncomfortable to consider addressing God with a term of childlike endearment, like DaDa or Abba? I'll admit, it makes me uncomfortable. What is it about you and me that makes us uncomfortable with this?

- How will you introduce or embolden your ways of beginning your prayers by praying your faith? What does or might this look like in your praying? Do other texts come to mind to lift up as prayers of faith?
- What about this movement of faith to hope to love in this prayer of Gethsemane? Am I imposing this onto the prayer or is it emanating like revelation from the prayer?

The Third Prayer of the Cross: The Forgiveness Prayer

61

LUKE 23:32–34 | Two other men, both criminals, were also led out with him to be executed. When they came to the place called the Skull, they crucified him there, along with the criminals—one on his right, the other on his left. Jesus said, "Father, forgive them, for they do not know what they are doing." And they divided up his clothes by casting lots.

Consider This

There's something about '80s songs that just won't leave you alone. And though so many of them were completely forgettable, history seems to vindicate them by making them more ubiquitous with each passing year. In a sea of curiously meaningless songs, some lyrics rise up out of all that smutty sentiment like islands of truth. One of those is Don Henley's song "The Heart of the Matter." The long and short of the song is this: the heart of the matter is forgiveness.

It brings us to the third prayer of the cross, the Forgiveness Prayer. We see the prayer only in Luke's gospel. It happens after all the violence and as he is lifted on the cross between the two others history knows only as "the criminals." Jesus prays: "*Father, forgive them, for they do not know what they are doing.*"

I see something for the first time in this text today. I always read this before as an act of Jesus forgiving his executors. He's not. Jesus is not dealing with his tormentors here. He is praying for them. He speaks not to them but to God.

"Father, forgive them, for they do not know what they are doing."

Permit me to test what may be an obvious insight. Forgiveness begins with God, not with us. In the Disciples' Prayer, Jesus teaches us to pray, "Forgive us our sins as we forgive those who sin against us." So critical is this prayer he comes back around at the end of it with this admonition: "For if you forgive other people when they sin against you, your heavenly Father will also forgive you. But if you do not forgive others their sins, your Father will not forgive your sins" (Matt. 6:14–15).

Unforgiveness creates a barrier not only in our relationship with other people but in our relationship with God. In fact, according to Jesus, our peace with God depends on our peace with other people. And, of course, we are able to forgive others because God has first forgiven us. Forgiveness is the heart of the matter.

Forgiveness can be so challenging for so many of us. We have endured wrongs and injustices that in so many cases seem unforgivable. Let me pose three observations.

In many, if not most, cases, the offenses people commit against us are not about us. They are about them. They come from their brokenness, immaturity, or infirmity. Broken people break people and they tend not to discriminate about who.

In a similar way, extending them forgiveness is not about them but us. Forgiveness is an act of grace, which by definition means it is undeserved favor.

Because forgiveness comes from God, it makes sense, especially in the difficult cases, to pray with Jesus. Rather than trying to forgive them directly, we can pray, *"Father, forgive them, for they do not know what they are doing."*

And what exactly is forgiveness? Forgiveness does not mean forgetting. It does not mean everything is okay. It does not necessarily mean a change of mind or heart toward the offender. It does not mean one's feelings have changed toward the offender. Forgiveness means one makes the willful decision to not retaliate against the offender. It takes time, but forgiveness means to cease fighting back whether actively, passively, passive-aggressively, personally, or communally.

A final clarification—forgiveness is not reconciliation. While reconciliation is bilateral, forgiveness is unilateral. Many never move toward forgiveness for fear it will require them to reconcile with the one who harmed them. This is not so. Holding on to unforgiveness may hurt the person from whom it is withheld, but it kills the one who holds on to it. Unforgiveness is like drinking poison and expecting it to kill the other person. It only kills you.

Finally, note the primary context for the working out of forgiveness is in prayer. We see it in the Disciples' Prayer and the Forgiveness Prayer of the Cross.

And when we get down to the heart of the matter, this is what the cross is all about: forgiveness.

The Prayer

Almighty, ascended Lord Jesus Christ, you are high and exalted yet nearer than our breath. Thank you for your forgiveness. Awaken me to grasp the depth of my need for forgiveness. Awaken me to grasp the breadth of the reality of my forgiveness. And awaken me to the grace you give me to forgive others. Right here, Jesus. Right now, Jesus. Amen.

The Questions

- Do you struggle to forgive other people? Why is that?
- How do you understand that unforgiveness hurts the one who cannot forgive?
- Have you ever considered how people's offenses toward us are more about them than us? What might it mean to take offenses less personally in light of this?

RIGHT HERE. RIGHT NOW.

The Fourth Prayer of the Cross: The Forsakenness Prayer

62

MARK 15:33–34 | At noon, darkness came over the whole land until three in the afternoon. And at three in the afternoon Jesus cried out in a loud voice, *"Eloi, Eloi, lema sabachthani?"* (which means "My God, my God, why have you forsaken me?").

Consider This

The feeling of being forsaken by God is a different thing from the reality of being forsaken by God. The former is a real experience. The latter is simply not real.

Did the Father, in an act of wrath, turn his face away from his Son as he suffered death on the cross? The idea has become something of a theological dogma in modern times. Though this text says nothing of the sort, nor can any other support of this claim be found elsewhere in Scripture without significant interpretive gymnastics, the idea continues to make its way into our songs and sermons. If someone can support the argument I would be glad to hear it.

The God in whom we believe, whom we call "Our Father," forsakes neither his creation nor his creatures, and especially not his image-bearers, and certainly not his Son. Consider this word from the psalmist.

> Where can I go from your Spirit?
>> Where can I flee from your presence?
> If I go up to the heavens, you are there;
>> if I make my bed in the depths, you are there.
> If I rise on the wings of the dawn,
>> if I settle on the far side of the sea,
> even there your hand will guide me,
>> your right hand will hold me fast.
> If I say, "Surely the darkness will hide me
>> and the light become night around me,"
> even the darkness will not be dark to you;
>> the night will shine like the day,
>> for darkness is as light to you. (Ps. 139:7–12)

Or how about this word from Paul:

> For I am convinced that neither death nor life, neither angels nor demons, neither the present nor the future, nor any powers, neither height nor depth, nor anything else in all creation, will be able to separate us from the love of God that is in Christ Jesus our Lord. (Rom. 8:38–39)

Still, Jesus prays this fourth prayer of the cross, the Forsakenness Prayer, "Eloi, Eloi, lema sabachthani?"

We have a hard time accepting this prayer. We don't want to let it stand. We need to put a theological framework of sin and wrath around it. Many suggest Jesus, in citing the first verse of Psalm 22, means to signal the whole of the psalm, which is far more hopeful in its overall outlook.

Why can't we let it stand? Why can't we accept the reality that Jesus really did experience the feeling of being forsaken by God? Jesus took on the fullness of the human experience, which includes the experience of feeling forsaken by God.

So many people live in abject poverty, facing intractable suffering and grave injustices and incurable diseases and enduring unimaginable losses. They feel forsaken by God. To enter into their lives is to share in the felt experience of their forsakenness. In fact, in so many cases, only in our going to them might they experience God's real presence.

In the years following Teresa of Calcutta's death, against her wishes, her secret journals came into public view. They reveal that over the last fifty years of her life she experienced an almost unbroken sense of being forsaken by God. It began almost precisely at the point which she shifted her work to serve among the poorest of the poor in Calcutta. Characteristic of these writings is the following excerpt that comes from a letter she wrote to a spiritual advisor and confidant: "[But] as for me, the silence and the emptiness is so great, that I look and do not see,—Listen and do not hear—the tongue moves [in prayer] but does not speak . . . I want you to pray for me— that I let Him have [a] free hand."

Forsakenness is a real experience and it can be occasioned by very real conditions. To be forsaken by God, however, is not possible. Perhaps this is why Jesus elevates to the level of eternal judgment the care of those who face the conditions and feelings of forsakenness: "For I was hungry and you fed me. I was thirsty and you gave me something to drink" (see Matthew 25).

It makes sense, doesn't it? The more we enter into the experience of those who feel forsaken, the more we will share their experience, even with our faith in tow. This is what God does because this is what love does.

So what of this Forsakenness Prayer.

"Eloi, Eloi, lema sabachthani?" *(My God, my God, why have you forsaken me?)*

What might it mean to enter into the experience of those in the world today who are themselves praying these words, whether with their lips or their lives? We feel sympathy for those experiencing forsakenness, and it might evoke our pity, but little else. Could we open ourselves to empathy, even divine empathy? What if this prayer is itself a small way of entering in?

Here's a challenge. Go into your prayer room, close the door, and prepare to enter into the Forsakenness Prayer. Invite the Holy Spirit to stir in you the remembrance of someone who is facing the experience of feeling forsaken by God. Perhaps you know this person. Perhaps the person is nameless and even faceless to you. It needs to be a person, though, and not a group. Hold that person in your mind and heart, and speak to God, not so much on their behalf but as it might be if you were actually them. Though you may want to pray for them in a lot of different ways, for the sake of this challenge, limit yourself to praying these words as them.

"Eloi, Eloi, lema sabachthani?" *(My God, my God, why have you forsaken me?)*

It will take saying it a number of times before you are praying. I will admit, though this is an edgy way of praying, it is a deeply intercessory way of prayer.

The Prayer

Almighty, ascended Lord Jesus Christ, you are high and exalted yet nearer than our breath. Thank you for being with us, really with us. Give me the courage and the grace to learn to be with others, in ways that I may not be comfortable with, in ways like you are with them. Right here, Jesus. Right now, Jesus. Amen.

The Questions

- How have you related to this Forsakenness Prayer in the past? Any experience with it?
- Have you ever experienced a sense of being forsaken by God? What was that like? How did you get through it?
- Will you take this challenge issued to enter into the Forsakenness Prayer, in the place of someone who is going through this dark place? If not, why not?

The Fifth Prayer of the Cross: The Abandonment Prayer

63

LUKE 23:44–46 | It was now about noon, and darkness came over the whole land until three in the afternoon, for the sun stopped shining. And the curtain of the temple was torn in two. Jesus called out with a loud voice, "Father, into your hands I commit my spirit." When he had said this, he breathed his last.

Consider This

Life always happens on two planes simultaneously. Those two planes are on earth and in heaven. There is the clear sense of unfolding events and there is the deeper meaning. We see it in dramatic fashion on Good Friday. On earth, we see the standard administration of a first-century death penalty. More unusually, we see a solar eclipse and an earthquake. We see the base coarseness of the human race as they hurl insults at this Galilean peasant. Even the criminals who flanked him insulted him. On earth, there is nothing religious or holy or sacred or anything of the sort happening.

In heaven—which, mind you, is not somewhere in the distance, but right here, right now—something altogether different is taking place. We behold a conversation taking place between the Father and the Son. From what we can perceive, there are five things the Son says to the Father over the course of these proceedings. At the risk of confining them to our own thin, conventional categories, we call them the prayers of the cross. They are, in fact, inexhaustible wells of divine revelation. They show us the way of heaven in the face of trial and tribulation on earth.

Today we come to the fifth and final prayer of the cross— which we will call the Abandonment Prayer.

"Father, into your hands I commit my spirit."

On earth, this scene playing out on the outskirts of Jerusalem looks like a travesty of justice with Jesus of Nazareth as the victim. He refuses this role, opting instead for the story of willful love, of costly obedience, of no matter what, win or lose, I belong to you, Father.

"Father, into your hands I commit my spirit."

We see the essence and contours of this final prayer of the cross woven throughout the other four.

The Glory Prayer

"Now my soul is troubled, and what shall I say? 'Father, save me from this hour'? No, it was for this very reason I came to this hour. Father, glorify your name!" (John 12:27–28)

The Gethsemane Prayer

"Abba, Father," he said, "everything is possible for you. Take this cup from me. Yet not what I will, but what you will." (Mark 14:36)

The Forgiveness Prayer

Jesus said, "Father, forgive them, for they do not know what they are doing." (Luke 23:34)

The Forsakenness Prayer

And at three in the afternoon Jesus cried out in a loud voice, *"Eloi, Eloi, lema sabachthani?"* (which means "My God, my God, why have you forsaken me?"). (Mark 15:34)

Far from the victim of grave injustice, Jesus is the champion of eternal victory. The same is true in our lives with all our little crosses. There is the thing that is happening. Then there is the bigger thing unfolding. We see on earth but we walk by faith in heaven. As we navigate our crosses with the way being lit by these great beacon prayers of his cross, God works out his purposes and plans.

The mark of maturity in this looks like a decreasing of so much complaining about our crosses to others and an increasing of our consecration to God in the midst of them. This Abandonment Prayer is a prayer of bold, beautiful trust.

If you will permit me a bit of a trite irreverence, this Abandonment Prayer is the secret sauce of the whole thing.

"Father, into your hands I commit my spirit."

Allow me to address many of you personally and directly with this charge: Christian, you belong to Jesus. The Word of God exhorts you without compromise:

> Since, then, you have been raised with Christ, set your hearts on things above, where Christ is, seated at the right hand of God. Set your minds on things above, not on earthly things. For you died, and your life is now hidden with Christ in God. (Col. 3:1–3)

What you now face is hard, unfair, and even wrong and unjust. Renounce your victimhood and take up your cross. Boldly claim the following reality: "I have been crucified with Christ and I no longer live, but Christ lives in me. The life I now live in the body, I live by faith in the Son of God, who loved me and gave himself for me" (Gal. 2:20).

Abandon yourself to him again and again and again until the old you is no more and only Jesus remains. All of creation waits for this person to be revealed. It has already begun. The way is the cross. The path is descent. The secret is abandonment. The joy is eternal. He is getting you where he wants you, though the path seems wrong. It always does.

Though you are tired, weak, and utterly incapable of facing the looming crosses ahead, you are a champion by the grace of God and the cross of Jesus. Never forget it, and always remind me. Pray it boldly now: *"Father, into your hands I commit my spirit."*

The Prayer

Almighty, ascended Lord Jesus Christ, you are high and exalted yet nearer than our breath. Thank you for showing me the hidden way of love is the secret yet public way of the cross. Save me from weak resignation that I might be filled with the Spirit's power, which is love's abandon. Right here, Jesus. Right now, Jesus. Amen.

The Questions

- Which prayer of the cross are you most identifying with these days? Why? How is it leading you?
- Do you have any experience with intentionally praying the Abandonment Prayer? How will you grow in that experience?

- Do you struggle with being a victim? Let me ask it another way. Do you spend a lot of time complaining about other people and their defeating impact on you?

64 The Real Lord's Prayer, Part One

JOHN 17:1–10 | After Jesus said this, he looked toward heaven and prayed:

"Father, the hour has come. Glorify your Son, that your Son may glorify you. For you granted him authority over all people that he might give eternal life to all those you have given him. Now this is eternal life: that they know you, the only true God, and Jesus Christ, whom you have sent. I have brought you glory on earth by finishing the work you gave me to do. And now, Father, glorify me in your presence with the glory I had with you before the world began.

"I have revealed you to those whom you gave me out of the world. They were yours; you gave them to me and they have obeyed your word. Now they know that everything you have given me comes from you. For I gave them the words you gave me and they accepted them. They knew with certainty that I came from you, and they believed that you sent me. I pray for them. I am not praying for the world, but for those you have given me, for they are yours. All I have is yours, and all you have is mine. And glory has come to me through them."

Consider This

Finally, we come to the ninth prayer of Jesus, the real Lord's Prayer. Biblical interpreters commonly refer to this prayer as Jesus' High Priestly Prayer.

Among all of Jesus' prayers, I find this one harder to appropriate in my own praying. It is Jesus' prayer and one he prays in a truly unique way. While it may not lend itself to a model for our praying, there are elements here that will inform our prayers.

We come to the end of the prayers only to discover they lead us back to the starting place. For starters, note how Jesus rehearses the fundamental fundamental in this conversation with his Father.

"Now this is eternal life: that they know you, the only true God, and Jesus Christ, whom you have sent."

Remember, the big change most of us need is not from less prayer to more prayer, which can be occasioned by making technical changes at the level of our practice. We need transformative change. We need to make the shift from the whole idea of a better prayer life to the consuming reality of a life of prayer.

It is not so much about asking for this and that as it is walking in close abiding fellowship with God: Father, Son, and Holy Spirit. Eternal life means walking with God in a life of prayer.

"For I gave them the words you gave me and they accepted them."

The most prominent word in the prayer appears fourteen times in one form or another: *gave*. The value system of the world runs by reciprocity. Reciprocity means a form of exchange that moves backward and forward. You scratch my back, I'll scratch yours. It works along the same lines of debts and credits.

The kingdom of God does not work by reciprocity. It moves by generosity. It is not backward and forward but downward and upward. Prayer moves us into the realm of giving and receiving. God will be neither our debtor nor our creditor. God will be God. The gospel of our God is extraordinarily and extravagantly generous beyond our wildest imagination. Jesus Christ is the generosity of God.

"I have brought you glory on earth by finishing the work you gave me to do."

The second most prominent word in the prayer, appearing no less than nine times, is *glory*. Generosity is a downward movement. Glory is the upward movement. God freely gives to us. His aim is not so we would give something back to him, but freely give to others. As the generosity of God becomes our generosity toward others, the glory goes up.

God is not so much glorified by our saying or singing "glory to God," as when our giving is filled with God's generosity. People will thank us, but they will know beyond knowing there is far more than us to thank. Glory comes when our gratitude for God's generosity becomes our generosity toward others. It is in our life of prayer where we remember and rehearse this generosity. Note how Jesus does it: *"All I have is yours, and all you have is mine."*

If we could wrap our minds, hearts, souls, and strength around these eleven words, everything would change. I don't mean agree with them or assent to them or otherwise run them up the flagpole and salute them. I mean own them. Eat them. Stake your life upon them.

"All I have is yours, and all you have is mine."

And by all means, make them your prayer, for these words are themselves the very bedrock of prayer. The power of our prayers will grow as the potency of our faith in this truth deepens.

Start by saying them with me now.

"All I have is yours, and all you have is mine."

Out loud!

"All I have is yours, and all you have is mine."

The Prayer

Almighty, ascended Lord Jesus Christ, you are high and exalted yet nearer than our breath. Thank you for this deep truth you revealed to us in your prayer to Abba Father. All I have is yours, and all you have is mine. Thank you that it is as true for us as it is for you. Right here, Jesus. Right now, Jesus. Amen.

The Questions

- "All I have is yours, and all you have is mine." On a scale of 1 to 10, with 10 being the highest, rate your level of faith in this truth.

- "Glory comes when our gratitude for God's generosity becomes our generosity toward others." What do you make of the connections between generosity and gratitude and glory? How do you see that working itself out in a practical way?
- How are you making the shift from a prayer life to a life of prayer?

65 | The Real Lord's Prayer, Part Two

JOHN 17:11–19 | "I will remain in the world no longer, but they are still in the world, and I am coming to you. Holy Father, protect them by the power of your name, the name you gave me, so that they may be one as we are one. While I was with them, I protected them and kept them safe by that name you gave me. None has been lost except the one doomed to destruction so that Scripture would be fulfilled.

"I am coming to you now, but I say these things while I am still in the world, so that they may have the full measure of my joy within them. I have given them your word and the world has hated them, for they are not of the world any more than I am of the world. My prayer is not that you take them out of the world but that you protect them from the evil one. They are not of the world, even as I am not of it. Sanctify them by the truth; your word is truth. As you sent me into the world, I have sent them into the world. For them I sanctify myself, that they too may be truly sanctified."

Consider This

In my experience over the course of my life, I would estimate that 90 percent of the prayer requests and prayers I have heard have been about keeping someone or some group of people safe. The others have been related to cancer. Whether people follow Jesus or even believe in God, when they come face-to-face with their vulnerability they become desperate for security and protection.

We realize our vulnerability and need for protection, yet we are far more vulnerable than we even realize. The world is a dangerous place. I have never noticed until now the emphasis Jesus places on protection in his high priestly prayer.

"I will remain in the world no longer, but they are still in the world, and I am coming to you. Holy Father, protect them by the power of your name . . ."

The world is a dangerous place, especially for the followers of Jesus. It is dangerous because it has the capacity to absolutely neutralize and eviscerate our witness and effectiveness as Christians. This is why Jesus leads us in the Disciples' Prayer to say, "Lead us not into temptation."

The world is a dangerous place, especially for those followers of Jesus who are making a real play with their lives for the kingdom of God and against the evil one. The world is not so dangerous on this count because of its seductive temptations (though they be ever-present) but because of the nature of Satanic treachery. This is why Jesus leads us in the Disciples' Prayer to say, "Deliver us from the evil one."

"My prayer is not that you take them out of the world but that you protect them from the evil one."

Satan is real. And if you aren't under attack or drawing enemy fire in some form or fashion, chances are you aren't in the real game. It's interesting how a lot of people consider their financially prosperous and relatively pain-free lives a sign of God's blessing. Certainly it can be, but in the cases I'm thinking of, these people are not even in the stadium, much less on the playing field.

In the prayer, Jesus gets at how we are protected from the evil one.

"They are not of the world, even as I am not of it."

Though it may be a cliché it is a solidly biblical one: If we would be protected from the evil one, we must learn to live "in the world but not of the world." Why? Because there is no protection for living of the world. To live in the world and of the world is to live in a state of exposure and vulnerability. It does not mean that God has withdrawn his protection as much as we have run out of bounds. We have left the perimeter of his protection. It makes sense that Jesus would take his prayer a step further:

"Sanctify them by the truth; your word is truth."

We are not immune from attack anywhere at any time, but attacks can be weathered and withstood as we remain in the protective perimeter of the truth of the Word of God. To *sanctify* means "to set apart as holy unto the Lord." God does this in us and for us through the truth of his Word. There is a form of false holiness that tries to withdraw from the world. The strategy of not being of the world for them means not being in the world.

The way of Jesus, which is the way of the cross, is to press deeper and deeper into the world while becoming less and less of the world. This is the meaning of true holiness. False holiness looks like being set apart *from* the world. True holiness looks like being set apart right in the midst of the world. The impulse of false holiness is to protect oneself from the world. The instinct of true holiness is to trust God for protection in the world.

We have all the resources of the Word, the Spirit, the church, and the kingdom. By these we are sanctified, equipped, preserved, held, kept, strengthened, empowered, healed, restored, emboldened, and, yes, protected. And all of this to such a degree we can stand with the saints (a.k.a. the holy ones) brandishing our scars and declaring, "We are hard pressed on every side, but not crushed; perplexed, but not in despair; persecuted, but not abandoned; struck down, but not destroyed" (2 Cor. 4:8–9).

Let's put a pin in it for today and finish the race tomorrow with part 3 of the Real Lord's Prayer, which will conclude our Daily Text prayer series.

The Prayer

Almighty, ascended Lord Jesus Christ, you are high and exalted yet nearer than our breath. We are desperate for your protection. Forgive me for all the ways I protect myself. Grace me to trust your protection. And teach me the way of being sanctified by the truth of your Word. Right here, Jesus. Right now, Jesus. Amen.

The Questions

- How much of your praying is consumed with concerns of safety and security of yourself and others?
- Have you experienced what it means to be under the attack of the evil one? What do you think merited that attack or drew his fire? How did you withstand it?
- What is your experience of being sanctified by the truth of God's Word? How has or is God's Word revealing your blind spots and vulnerabilities to attack?

66 The Real Lord's Prayer, Part Three

JOHN 17:20–26 | "My prayer is not for them alone. I pray also for those who will believe in me through their message, that all of them may be one, Father, just as you are in me and I am in you. May they also be in us so that the world may believe that you have sent me. I have given them the glory that you gave me, that they may be one as we are one—I in them and you in me—so that they may be brought to complete unity. Then the world will know that you sent me and have loved them even as you have loved me.

"Father, I want those you have given me to be with me where I am, and to see my glory, the glory you have given me because you loved me before the creation of the world.

"Righteous Father, though the world does not know you, I know you, and they know that you have sent me. I have made you known to them, and will continue to make you known in order that the love you have for me may be in them and that I myself may be in them."

Consider This

We began this prayer series with the ascension of Jesus to the right hand of God to take up his work as the chief intercessor of heaven and earth. We end with his intercession for us as recorded in his High Priestly Prayer. And what a prayer it is.

"My prayer is not for them alone. I pray also for those who will believe in me through their message, that all of them may be one, Father, just as you are in me and I am in you. May they also be in us so that the world may believe that you have sent me."

It's pretty interesting. He doesn't pray for us to evangelize the whole world. He doesn't pray for us to end poverty or create world peace or otherwise save the planet. He is not even praying for us to make disciples of all nations. To be sure, these are all top-level concerns, but when Jesus has the opportunity to say a lengthy prayer in the hearing of a soon-to-be apostle who would write it down for all posterity, he doesn't pray for the kinds of things typically characterizing our prayers. He prays for our relationships with each other. He prays, *"that all of them may be one, Father, just as you are in me and I am in you."*

In other words, Jesus prays for my relationship with you to have the self-same quality and essence of his relationship to the Father. Taking it a step further, he adds to the prayer for us, saying, *"May they also be in us."*

Why this? Again, he makes it pretty clear: *"so that the world may believe that you have sent me."*

If I'm reading this right, according to Jesus, the mission of God to save the world depends on the quality of relationships among his followers. It makes sense. A few minutes earlier, after washing his disciples' feet, Jesus told them, "A new command I give you: Love one another. As I have loved you, so you must love one another. By this everyone will know that you are my disciples, if you love one another" (John 13:34–35).

"So that the world may believe that you have sent me."

Doesn't it stand to reason that Jesus' major prayer focus to the present-day centers around the relationships among his followers? If this is so, doesn't it follow that our major prayer focus should center around our relationships within the body of Christ? After all, this matter of peace in our relationships is a major focus of the Disciples' Prayer.

We exert so much prayer and expend so much energy around our mission efforts to do this, that, and the other to the end of seeking God's kingdom on earth as it is in heaven. Might Jesus be saying he will take care of expanding his kingdom in the world if we will focus on seeking his kingdom within our relationships in the body of Christ?

It's yet another reason we focus so much of our mission bandwidth at Seedbed to calling the followers of Jesus to band together. It just may be the most significant sowing for a great awakening we can do.

The Prayer

Almighty, ascended Lord Jesus Christ, you are high and exalted yet nearer than our breath. Thank you for this powerful prayer you prayed for us. Thank you that you have been praying for us ever since. Draw us into the gravity of your praying and, in doing so, draw us together into the kind of relationship you enjoy with our Father—so that the world will believe. Right here, Jesus. Right now, Jesus. Amen.

The Questions

- Are we focusing our sense of mission as the church in the wrong direction?
- How do the broken relationships in your life harm or compromise your witness to others?
- Is there a broken relationship in your life that needs to become front and center in your praying agenda?